PA WALLACE

A STORY OF MISSION IN SIERRA LEONE 1949-1987

Recalled by Rev S Leslie Wallace MBE, CR

By Ken Todd

Published by S K Todd
in association with
Methodist Missionary Society (Ireland), Aldersgate House, Belfast
and
The Methodist Church Sierra Leone, George Street, Freetown

©2012 S K Todd
All rights reserved
ISBN 978-0-9571332-0-4

Designed by April Sky Design, Newtownards
www.aprilsky.co.uk

Printed by W&G Baird Limited, Antrim

Rev S Leslie Wallace ministered in Sierra Leone from 1949 to 1987 including a short time in the Gambia. He was President of the Methodist Church, Sierra Leone for three periods.

Rev S K Todd ministered in Sierra Leone from 1966 to 1978, is a graduate of the University of Sierra Leone and a former President of the Methodist Church in Ireland.

FOREWORD

President of the Methodist Church, Sierra Leone

I consider it a great honour to be invited to write this foreword to the publication of these recollections of our dear and revered father of mission in Sierra Leone, the Rev Samuel Leslie Wallace. Reverend S L Wallace came to Sierra Leone as a young minister in 1949 and gave sacrificial service to the people of this nation for nearly forty years. He served the Methodist Church Sierra Leone with love and dedication. It was the love of God that he experienced in Christ Jesus that motivated his service and that was made manifest to all who came across him in the course of his ministry. He is very much appreciated and greatly loved for his charm and hard work.

It was my privilege to meet Pa Wallace (as we fondly refer to him) when I decided to candidate for the ordained ministry of the Methodist Church. I approached him in his capacity as President of Conference and was warmly received as we discussed the procedures. He accompanied me through my probationary period and contributed to whatever achievement, by the grace of God, I have made in ministry. I am not alone in this for a good number of ministers in the Methodist Church Sierra Leone today can pay like tribute to our revered father in God.

Reverend Leslie Wallace, an Irish missionary, has a strong commitment to the Kingdom of God and made such an appeal to the people of Sierra Leone, not just the Methodists but in the ecumenical circles as well. He served as President of the United Christian Council (now Council of Churches in Sierra Leone – CCSL) and made his mark on the ecumenical family in Sierra Leone.

His commitment to prophetic ministry coupled with his frank approach to difficult issues earned him the respect of the government of Sierra Leone and his engagement with State House on pertinent issues was taken seriously. I can recall such engagement in the students' unrest of 1977 and labour unrest of 1980 and the lead role he played in the advocacy for prison reforms in Sierra Leone. He spoke on behalf of the oppressed and downtrodden.

It was no surprise that at the death of the Rev P A J Williams on his first year of service as President of the Methodist Church Sierra Leone, Pa Wallace was not only called upon to succeed him in his capacity of Immediate Past President, but was overwhelmingly voted for the second time at the ensuing Conference.

We envisage the great value that this publication offers particularly to the Church in Sierra Leone. It is a useful resource for the formation of both our local preachers and ministers. It is also a record of the valuable input of a great man of God. This generation of Methodists in Sierra Leone will always remember him; but more so, the story needs to be passed on to generations after us.

In our hearts we hold Rev S L Wallace dearly. May the blessings of God continue to rest upon him.

Rt Rev Arnold C Temple
(President, Methodist Church, Sierra Leone) November 2011

President-designate of the Methodist Church in Ireland

It gives me great pleasure to write a word of introduction and commendation of this work on the life of my very dear friend, Rev S Leslie Wallace. I first met Leslie in the Mourne Grange Missionary Summer School in 1972, a few weeks before I first travelled to Sierra Leone. Having said that, my awareness of him went back to my childhood, as his brother Frank was a leading member of my own church in Regent Street, Newtownards, Co. Down and indeed for many years was my Sunday School superintendent.

Meeting Leslie for the first time, I got the impression of a very humble, self-effacing man who never seemed to want to be in the limelight. What a different picture I got in Sierra Leone! Here was a man who was a statesman and churchman and who was deeply revered and respected by all who knew him and even by those who did not share his Christian faith. Members of the Islamic community saw in him a man they could trust and one whose motives sought the greatest good for all.

Leslie has always been interested in the good of the whole person. He has been supportive of development projects in education, medicine, agriculture and industry, but behind them all has been the motivating factor to see people live lives to the full in Christ Jesus. It was my very great privilege to have Leslie as a colleague in his retirement while I was minister of his church in Carnalea, Bangor, Co. Down from 1998 to 2006. He was ever willing to help in the preaching, always so encouraging of my work. Visits to him always lasted longer than intended, as he had such wise and interesting things to say.

For years many of us have wanted to see the vast store of things held in his head committed to paper for the benefit of generations to come. I am very pleased that Ken Todd has risen to this challenge, and all who read this biography will be grateful to him. Of course, it is the case that many books could not contain all that this dear servant of God has achieved, but at least here is a sample of them. May they be an inspiration to all who seek the extension of Christ's Kingdom as Leslie has done throughout his long and full life of arduous service for his Master.

Rev Kenneth R Lindsay
(President-designate of the Methodist Church in Ireland)
November 2011

PREFACE

The life-story of Leslie Wallace is a collection of many stories which centre upon 39 years as a mission partner in Sierra Leone, West Africa. He may be 90 years young yet his stories are clear and Sierra Leone and its peoples are held dear in his heart. It is no wonder that many in Sierra Leone like to think that his initials 'S L' refer to their country. He is often referred to as 'Pa Wallace' which is a term of respect and endearment.

These pages are written in response to frequent requests from the Methodist Church in Sierra Leone. There are few enough records of this vigorous era in the history of the church with some documentation destroyed in the rebel war of 1991-2002. This record is like an act of a drama which is unfolding according to God's direction. The central plot of this drama is found in the words of the Lord Jesus Christ who said: "I will build my church, and the gates of hell shall not prevail against it" (Matthew 16:18).

The first twelve years of Leslie's missionary service were under British Colonial rule and the remaining twenty-seven years were lived in an independent Sierra Leone. He worked for a Kingdom that transcended both. Hundreds of expatriate people left the country at Independence in 1961. Leslie did not flinch at the wind of change which was blowing. He was devoid of colonialist or neo-colonialist attitudes because his worldview was Christian and without prejudice. The stories are many and as the Queen of Sheba said: "the half has not been told." It is hoped that these stories will open a window on an era of expanding mission. The Wolof proverb heard during Leslie's brief spell in The Gambia is apt: "If you are familiar with the beginning, the end will not give trouble." We first met in 1966 in Belfast when I was preparing for missionary service in Sierra Leone. He told me to get a copy of the Mende Bible and hymnbook as well as a copy of Brown's Double Entry Book-keeping Manual. It was a reminder that a minister should be a good steward. This book contains the recollections of a good steward in the household of God.

I have taken the liberty, in this bi-centenary year, of inserting an introduction in the form of a biographical note on the first official Wesleyan Methodist missionary to Africa, George Warren, who arrived in Freetown in November 1811. I hope this note will help set the scene for the ensuing record of mission.

Thank you to Verena Wallace, Sheila Johnston, Cecil Newell and Sahr Yambasu who have read the script and made helpful suggestions. I am grateful to my wife Frances for her assistance.

I apologise for any names which have been omitted and for any lapses of memory.

Ken Todd, Lisburn,
November 2011

Maps of Sierra Leone (above) and Ireland (right) to the same scale.

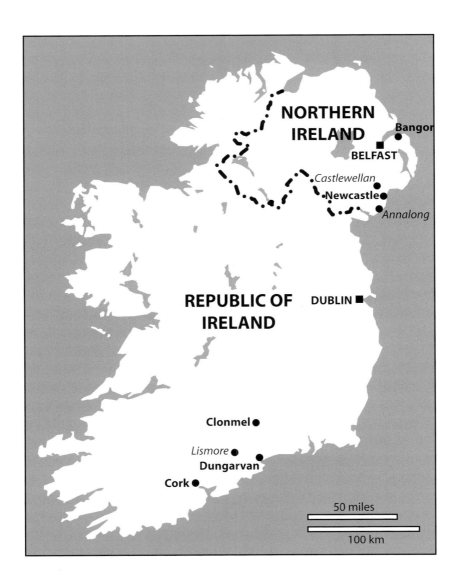

INTRODUCTION

FREETOWN

18
20 11

METHODIST
MISSION
SIERRA LEONE

Two hundred years ago on 12 November 1811, the first official Methodist missionaries to the Continent of Africa arrived in the West African country of Sierra Leone. In 1811 Rev Dr Thomas Coke, 'the Father of Methodist Missions', sent four English missionaries to Sierra Leone, a travelling preacher and three schoolteachers, two of whom were local preachers. The Wesleyan missionary preacher was George Warren. The teachers were Jonathan Raynor, John Healey and Thomas Hirst. Sadly, for such a key figure, we have not yet been able to discover the birthplace or birth date of George Warren, nor do we have a picture.

He was first stationed in Cardiff in 1807, followed by appointments in Kington (Shrewsbury), St Austell and later Helstone, Cornwall. Rev Dr Thomas Coke actually travelled to Helstone by stagecoach to recruit Mr Warren to open up the work in Africa and go to Sierra Leone where freed slaves had formed a new settlement on the coast. The parents of George Warren opposed their son's move and he wrote to them: "beseeching them by the blood of souls" not to hinder him from going. It was after his mother died that he was able to offer for Africa.

Warren and the three schoolteachers from Yorkshire were escorted to the docks in Liverpool by Dr Coke and three Liverpool Superintendents. We think that George Warren had just been ordained by Dr Coke prior to embarkation, since ordination was essential for overseas appointments although not yet agreed for Methodist preachers stationed at home. As far as we know the missionary four were single men. They sailed on 21st September 1811 on a brig which was aptly known as 'Traveller.' During the hazardous voyage they were pursued by a French privateer, possibly supporting the Napoleonic war effort, but escaped "by Providence" and arrived fifty-two days later in the settlement of Freetown in Sierra Leone on 12 November 1811.

They were warmly welcomed by the Governor and the Anglican chaplain and especially by Methodist members from the community of freed slaves who had already on their own initiative built a chapel to accommodate 400 people. The patient Methodists rejoiced that: "They now found the basis and authority for the Sacraments in their own chapel." Warren and his companions began learning the language, setting up schools and networking with local African chiefs and reaching out beyond the Colony area to the tribes of the hinterland. Invitations filtered through from as far away as Senegal and the Gold Coast. The Inaugural Conference of the Methodist Church in Sierra Leone wrote to the Missionary Society recalling the contribution of the early freed slaves who settled in Sierra Leone:

"When our fathers settled in this country in 1792 they brought with them 'that good thing which could not have been taken from them' - the gospel light. Slowly but surely and continuously this light developed into a blaze which spread down the Coast, bringing light to many. Today we are grateful to them and hold them in blessed remembrance."

The Methodists in Liverpool had donated school furniture as well as 200 Bibles and the Bible Society presented 25 Arabic Bibles, 25 English Bibles and 25 New Testaments. In a letter to his successor in Helstone, Warren confirms his sense of call from God and humbly prays for "wisdom and power from on high." He claimed that: "it was his intention to instruct them to read and write in English and to teach them how to be happy after death." There had been little orientation available for these pioneers so Dr Coke read travellers' tales and used Warren's letters and experiences to write a book which would serve as an orientation manual for later missionaries to Africa entitled: "An Interesting Narrative of a Mission sent to Sierra Leone, in Africa, by the Methodists in 1811, to which is prefixed, an account of the rise, progress, disasters, and present state of the Colony." The experience of

Warren and his school teacher companions in Sierra Leone no doubt helped in the creation of the Wesleyan Methodist Missionary Society which was later formalised in 1818. Methodist overseas missions work had begun in 1786 in Antigua. The Wesleyan Methodist Missionary Society was not legally established for another 32 years.

George Warren sadly lasted for only 8 months and 11 days and died of a fever, probably malaria, in Freetown on 23rd July 1812. His obituary includes the tribute:

"He laboured even more than would perhaps have been prudent even in his native country. The Lord blessed his labours, so that the congregation and society increased, and many souls were awakened and converted under his ministry. His death was sudden, and must, on that account have been afflictive to his friends, but that his constant walk with God, and his deep communion with the Father, and with His son Jesus Christ, were evident to all who knew him."

The mission of God is always costly. In 1828 six missionaries died in Sierra Leone in the course of that single year. A missionary preacher named Henry T Harte, who died in 1824, was buried in the grave of George Warren. Of the three original missionary schoolteachers, Jonathan Raynor returned to England in 1812 in ill health and was later stationed in the West Indies. John Healy and Thomas Hirst returned home in 1817 having begun a tradition of Methodist schooling which continues with vigour today.

The British and Irish Churches celebrate with the Methodist Church in Africa which continues to grow with an estimated 30 million Methodists throughout the continent. Methodists in Europe have much to learn from the life and witness of the African church.

Today in Freetown there is a Warren Memorial Chapel named after George Warren. More importantly, the seed that fell into the African ground 200 years ago bears a lasting fruit and the expressed vision of Dr Coke is being realised:

"...in the colony of Sierra Leone (we) hold out an example to future generations, which we hope, will be a blessing to millions yet unborn."

Ken Todd

CHAPTER 1

IRELAND - THE EARLY YEARS

Leslie with brother Ronnie 1933

Samuel Leslie Wallace was born on 24 March 1921 in Belfast, the second of four children born to Francis and Elizabeth Wallace. His siblings were Frank, Helen and Ronnie. The family belonged to the Presbyterian Shankhill Road Mission, Belfast. When they moved to the town of Bangor beside the sea they walked to a Presbyterian Church on their first Sunday in the town. A man wearing black formal clothes informed them that they were sitting in his seat. The caretaker moved them to another seat near to the side exit. On Monday, going to his work, Mr Wallace senior related this episode to a friend on the train. His friend invited him to Queen's Parade Methodist Church and assured him of a warm welcome. So it was that the Wallace family became Methodists and history would be made. Their home was God-fearing and devout and was filled with love for Christ and his Church. The parents commended their Saviour to the children.

Leslie continued his education at Bangor Central School, where he was a foundation pupil. He progressed to Bangor Technical School and Belfast Technical College where he qualified with City and Guilds in Typography and Graphic Arts and gained further qualifications with The Royal Society of Arts in English and Maths. His first job was at Dorman's firm as a printing apprentice. He worked for seven years in the printing trade and God's hand was surely in this training which would be of strategic use in a West African country.

As a youth he was a member of the Christian Endeavour and the Methodist Sunday School and he learned to take part in public prayers and readings in church. He served as a Warrant Officer in the 4th Bangor Company of the Boys' Brigade and learned the lessons of leadership.

It was at the Methodist Church that he met his future wife, Agnes Thompson, the only child of Robert and Elizabeth Thompson. Leslie and Agnes were converted at a Sunday evening service when they were teenagers. The preacher was Rev S T Nelson and five young people responded to the gospel appeal as the preacher explained the text, John 5:24. They were told that accepting Christ as their personal Saviour was only the beginning and that they should keep in step with God's Holy Spirit at all times. John 5:24 remained a favourite text of Leslie's: "Whoever hears my word and believes Him who sent me has eternal life and will not be condemned; he has crossed over from death to life."

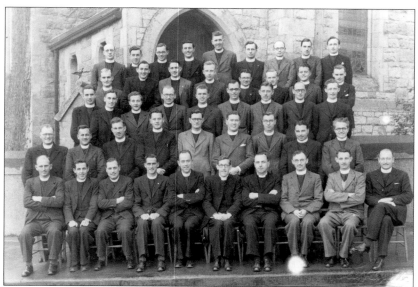

Junior Ministers' Convention at Clontarf, Dublin 1944

Preparation at home for a world church ministry overseas

While working as a printer he studied to become a Methodist local preacher. In 1942, encouraged by Rev Henry Armstrong, he began preaching at Carnalea Methodist Church, Bangor. During the war years he was a member of the Bangor Hospital stretcher team, serving in Belfast during the blitz. In 1942 he became a full time lay evangelist on the Newcastle circuit with special responsibility for Castlewellan and Annalong. He travelled by bicycle in the hilly terrain around the Mourne mountains. On one wet night he cycled to take an evening service in the little grey church in Castlewellan. He was soaked to the skin. Only the caretaker was present and he felt like going home to get dry. However, he conducted the service as in the presence God and at the end of it, the caretaker asked him: "Mr. Wallace, I have often wondered how I should go about being saved!" There and then the caretaker accepted Jesus Christ as personal Saviour. Leslie was so filled with joy that he never felt the rain on his way home.

The Methodist Church in Annalong was well-attended. The congregation was made up of farmers and the fishing community and was augmented by American soldiers. The Superintendent minister in Newcastle was Rev J Dwyer Kelly. This was during the time of the Second World War and in the course of his work as an evangelist he befriended some of the American soldiers who were stationed nearby. On occasions he teamed up with the USA army chaplains. This was another preparation for his time as Officiating Chaplain to the Armed Forces of Sierra Leone. One night while cycling along the coast road to Newcastle from Annalong after a service, he was arrested in a case of mistaken identity when the Special Forces were searching for an escaped prisoner who was thought to be wearing a greatcoat similar to that of the lay evangelist. Leslie could recount this experience when he would later serve as prison Chaplain to Pademba Road prison in Freetown, Sierra Leone.

He candidated for the Methodist Ministry in 1944 and was sent as a pre-collegiate probationer to Dublin at Ringsend on the Sandymount circuit. The church was lively with three Sunday Schools and three Christian Endeavour groups. Ringsend church had its own outdoor tennis court, adjacent to the church. The Superintendent minister at Sandymount was Rev Alfred Collins. After one year Leslie was sent to Dungarvan on the south coast of Ireland. The church building was 'an upper room' at the rear of Hadden's shop. Mr Siberry, the manager of the shop, prepared the church for worship. Leslie succeeded Rev Malcolm Redmond and lodged in the same private house where the landlady, a Roman Catholic, was well-versed in Methodist history and doctrine. Occasionally, it is told, she sprinkled a little holy water on the Methodist preacher as he went out the door. The work included Clonmel and Lismore.

After a year Leslie was sent for a few months to the city of Cork where he preached in Wesley Chapel in Patrick Street which had a high pulpit with so many steps that he felt near to heaven. He also preached at Military Road Methodist Church and at a large country house belonging to the Nicholson family who were farmers. This house was filled for worship each Sunday evening during summer months. As soon as the preacher had pronounced the benediction, tea and sandwiches and cakes instantly appeared and fifty people were fed.

It was while at Cork that he felt an inward impression on his soul to offer himself to the Methodist Missionary Society for overseas missions. Many of his contemporaries had courageously offered for service in the 1939-45 war although conscription was not compulsory in Northern Ireland. He felt moved to offer for service in the church overseas in order to extend Christ's Kingdom of love and right relationships amongst all people. It was a time when many hundreds of Irish Christians were serving as overseas missionaries. In his home town of Bangor, a Worldwide Missionary Convention had begun in 1936 and each year scores of young people were led to offer for missionary service at this Convention. This also had an impact on Leslie who in later years would be invited to address the Convention.

When he completed two years as a pre-collegiate probationer he went to Edgehill Theological College, Belfast, in 1946 and studied for three years under the principalship of Rev Dr W Northridge and the tutorship of Rev R Ernest Ker and Rev Richard Greenwood. Other students included Sydney Callaghan, Charles Eyre, Cecil Newell, Wilfred Agnew, Robin Smith, David Turtle, Jock Gordon, Brian Dougall, Jack McClintock, Wesley Gray, Joe McCrory, Jim McEvoy, Tom Sawyer, George Ferguson, Billy Nicoll and Martin Lyness. One of these would become an Army Deputy Chaplain General, three became

Back row L-R: Jim McEvoy; Jack McClintock; Martin Lyness; Joe McCrory. Middle row L-R: Sydney Callaghan; Wilfred Agnew; Brian Dougall; John Gordon; Cecil Newell; Billy Nichol. Front row L-R: David Turtle; Tom Sawyer; Rev R E Ker (Senior Tutor); Rev Dr W E Northridge (Principal); Rev Richard Greenwood (Tutor); Miss Thomas (Matron); Leslie Wallace.

President of the Methodist Church in Ireland and five would serve as missionaries in Burma, West Indies, Rhodesia and Sierra Leone.

At one point in their studies Dr Northridge suggested to the students that they should mingle with the Belfast public and record their observations. In this process the students played a prank on Sydney Callaghan. Sydney was from a wealthy Dublin family and was conscious of the need to empathise more with the poor. He dressed as a tramp one Saturday evening and played the violin (badly) to the queues of Belfast people waiting to enter the cinemas of Great Victoria Street. One of his fellow students, Jock McClintock, had a brother-in-law who was a policeman and arranged to have Sydney arrested and taken to Sandy Row police station where he was later released without charge. The Principal of the College was not amused.

Leslie was accepted as a missionary candidate while in College. Rev R E Ker had been a missionary lecturer in Uzakoli Theological College, Nigeria, and he guided Leslie's reading in preparation for overseas service. Because there were other missionary candidates, Edgehill also provided a short course in building construction, run by Mr Ferguson, a Belfast layman from the Sydenham congregation. He gave basic instructions on constructing simple buildings and explained cement mixtures for block making and foundations. This proved very useful when prospective missionaries were faced with the need to erect primary school buildings and manses. Mission House in London provided basic training in accountancy and book-keeping in a correspondence course directed by Mr Kitchener of the Finance Department. This course was valuable for a Circuit Superintendent and a future Secretary of Conference in Sierra Leone. Leslie was sent to the David Livingstone Medical College at Blackheath, London, where he learned first aid and basic dentistry. He later confessed that he never was an expert at pulling teeth.

It was helpful to be able to speak with a Methodist minister from Ireland, Rev Henry N Medd who, with his wife Alice, served in Segbwema, Sierra Leone, 1919-1928. Their story is interesting. In those days there were few roads and fewer vehicles. The Medds arrived in Freetown by ship and then transferred to a small boat which carried them and their loads up-river to Mattru Jong from whence they walked with porters carrying their baggage on their heads. They spent some time in Bandajuma Sowa in the south and eventually they arrived in Segbwema in the east where Mrs Alice Medd started a Maternity Clinic on the mission compound about 1920. This small clinic soon expanded to become the Wesley Guild Hospital Segbwema in 1930, later re-named the Nixon Memorial Methodist Hospital, Segbwema. The hospital owes its existence to Alice Medd. Some Segbwema girls have been named Alice down through the years. There were early superstitions about the midwifery practised by Mrs Medd and there was initial reluctance on the part of local Mende people to support the clinic. Later when Mrs Medd's clinic moved to the present hospital site, one of the first babies to be born was Kenneth P G Conteh who later became the first African Principal of Wesley Secondary School, Segbwema. His brave mother Lucia, a wonderful Christian lady, ignored the cries of the women of the town imploring her not to go to the hospital. Lucia was among the first Mende women who became nurses at Segbwema. These women, including a Sister Alice, played no small role in persuading Mende men and women who were used to traditional healing methods, to avail of the new health care services.

In the mission compound at Segbwema Rev H N Medd buried their only son who lived one month and died of malaria. When the Medds returned to Ireland, Henry Medd became known as 'Mende Medd' because he was always talking about the Mende people. It was during his time in Segbwema that the colonial government banned the practice of child-sacrifice.

Another retired Irish missionary, whom Leslie met at a missionary Summer School, was Sister Olly Robertson from Cork. Sister Robertson had served as a missionary nurse in Nigeria before she was sent to Segbwema where she did much to develop maternity services and became Sister Tutor of the nursing school. During the Second World War when there was no resident doctor for three years, she had to act as a Medical Superintendent and was required to perform emergency surgery. Some nurses who trained with Sister Robertson at the Royal Victoria Hospital in Belfast collected for a fund and from its provision, for many years, a prize was awarded to the best student nurse at Segbwema.

CHAPTER 2

SIERRA LEONE - ARRIVAL AND APPOINTMENT TO BUNUMBU

Arrival in Freetown

When Leslie was leaving home for Africa, his father, with other family members, knelt with him at the fireplace in their home and his father prayed for him. This was the practice each time Leslie would be returning to Sierra Leone after furlough. It was the custom for Belfast Christians to escort departing missionaries to the docks and pray with them on the quayside and sing the hymn: "God be with you till we meet again." At Liverpool Leslie sailed for Sierra Leone on board a cargo boat owned by Elder Dempster Lines. The journey took ten days, the ticket cost £49 and the ship called at Las Palmas before docking at Freetown on 1st September 1949. There was no facility for the large ship to dock in Freetown so it moored off the coast and the passengers clambered down the side of the ship to board a small barge which took them and their baggage to King Jimmy Wharf. Leslie recalled that the friendly welcome, the steamy humidity and the smell of fish in tropical heat were unforgettable first impressions. The baggage was carried on the head of porters through Freetown to the Methodist Church Headquarters building in 11 Gloucester Street, not far from the famous Cotton Tree where slaves were once sold and, after the abolition of the slave trade, were later released.

Leslie was greeted by the acting Chairman of District Rev W T Harris while Rev L W Juby was on leave. For five days in Freetown he purchased provisions and equipment and read material on things pertaining to Mende life and culture. At that time, the Freetown Peninsula was the Colony and the rest of the interior was the Protectorate. The life, language and culture of the people were different in the two areas. Methodism in the Colony (Freetown) area was different from Methodism in the Protectorate ('Committee') area. The Methodist Church in the colony formed the Sierra Leone District of the British Church, while Methodism in the Protectorate was governed directly by Mission House in London.

In Freetown the church was well organised. Class meetings met regularly for both young and old. Leaders meetings were active and choirs were well trained by skilled organists and choirmasters. At the first service on Sundays the order of morning prayer was used. The ordained ministry was made up of Creole ministers who were well educated at Fourah Bay College, affiliated to the University of Durham. Committed Christian lay people had a long history of vigorous leadership within the church. Freetown Methodism had Church primary schools with well-trained teachers and two excellent Secondary Schools, the Methodist Boys' High School and the Methodist Girls' High School. A Women's Work committee was very active both in church and community affairs. Local preachers were trained and active in fulfilling appointments throughout the District. They formed the Local Preachers Mutual Aid Association which included members of another branch of Methodism, the West African Methodist Church. Freetown Methodist worship was usually formal, using the prayer book and with robed choirs. The dress of the worshippers was also formal. Church buildings were substantial and several had stained glass windows. Zion Church in Wilberforce Street was built in 1792; College Chapel in Rawdon Street in 1809 and St John's Maroon Methodist Church was opened in 1818, not far from the Cotton Tree. The Maroons were freed slaves from Jamaica who arrived in Freetown in 1800 to join the freed Nova Scotian slaves in the settlement. The Nova Scotians evangelised many Maroons who then built their own church. The main wooden beams of St John's Maroon Methodist church incorporate up-ended beams from the hull of a former slave ship. It is a striking symbol of redemption. Methodism in the Colony area is thus steeped in long history. When George Warren and the first official Methodist missionaries arrived in the Freetown settlement in 1811, they already found a Methodist chapel which the freed slaves had constructed and which could seat 400 people. Before that, in 1792 there were 223 members of Methodist Society recorded for Freetown. From Sierra Leone, Methodism spread across West Africa.

Creole ministers occasionally served in the Protectorate, usually in chaplaincy roles to Creole communities along the railway line. Some sacrificed their life, such as the martyrs in Tikonko during the Hut Tax War in 1898. At that time innocent Creoles and some missionaries were slaughtered in many parts of the country, mistakenly regarded as collaborators with the Government after the Protectorate had been declared in 1896. The Creole Methodist martyrs at Tikonko were Mr Timothy Campbell, Mr Theo Roberts and Rev J C Johnston. Their bodies were thrown into the well on the mission compound. Later Rev A E Greensmith built a monument over the well, in their memory.

The early development of work in the Protectorate

The Methodist work in the Protectorate was more recent and tended to be led by missionaries. In England the major branches of Methodism had come together in 1932 to form The Methodist Church. The following year in 1933 in Sierra Leone, some Protestant missionary agencies met in Freetown. In a respectful arrangement or 'comity', they agreed not to overlap in the work of evangelisation. Present at the meeting were the leaders of the American Wesleyans, the Methodists, the United Brethren in Christ and the Evangelical United Brethren. We have not seen original documents of this historic meeting which had such a bearing on the evangelisation of the hinterland. Rev A E Dymond was one of the Methodist representatives. The discussion focussed on evangelism and church planting among different people groups in the language areas of Mende, Themne, Limba, Loko, Kono, Kissy and Sherbro. The American Wesleyans were allocated the North. They had a church in Pendembu in the east which they ceded to the Methodists in return for the handing over of Methodist work in the North. The Methodist Mission would work among the Mende and Kissy in the Eastern Province, in some parts of the Southern Province along the railway line, and in Bonthe Island. The Evangelical United Brethren went to the Southern Province and some parts of the Eastern Province including work among the Kono people. It was agreed that the missions would not compete in villages. However in larger centres like Bo, Bonthe, Kenema, Port Loko, Makeni or Magburaka, it was accepted that there could be an overlap. The Anglicans were mainly concentrated in Freetown and Bo and the Church Missionary Society had work in Port Loko in the North.

In the Protectorate, Methodist missionaries were stationed directly from London in Circuits, Bible Schools and Bunumbu Training College. Missionary doctors and nurses were appointed to the Methodist Hospital at Segbwema, later named the Nixon Memorial Methodist Hospital after its benefactor Alderman Nixon of Newcastle on-Tyne, an uncle of Rev Sidney Nixon Groves who later became the first Chairman of the Provincial District of the Methodist Church. Dr Mary Groves, his wife, worked as a doctor in both Kailahun and Kenema Districts. The medical and nursing personnel were responsible for training nurses, midwives and hospital administration staff. They helped develop village clinics and a nutrition centre, concentrating on mother and baby care, malnutrition and Lassa fever. The missionary minister was also manager of schools. Church buildings were mostly plain, often made of wattle and thatch. Worship services tended to be informal and evangelistic and people were being converted to Christ. Church planting was vigorous and was accompanied with educational and medical provision.

There was until 1951 a dichotomy between the Colony Church and the missionary work in the Protectorate or 'Committee Area'. The formation of the Mende Area Council was a step towards integration and a preparation for indigenous oversight of the church in the Protectorate Area. After 1951 the Synod area of the Colony began to receive minutes and reports from the Mende Area Council and exercise a duty of care for the work in the Protectorate. The Mende Area Council was laying the foundation for a Provincial Synod in a unified Conference, and it included lay representatives from the circuits. Teachers and catechists played an important part in the work of the Mende Area Council. Many gave valuable help in the committee for the translation of the Bible into the Mende language.

The Missionary Society in London was encouraging the promotion of evangelism, education and medicine in the hope of preparing up-country Methodism for indigenous leadership. Polygamy (properly *polygyny*) and sometimes alcoholism had hindered the appointment of men to be full members. Women's equality was a foreign concept and often women remained as 'seekers' or 'catechumens' for long periods of time. The appointment of Wesley Deaconesses and Women Workers to concentrate on the training of women for membership was acceptable to local customs and traditions. Advances were made in the training of women and girls in the Women's Training Centre, Segbwema and Njaluahun Methodist Girls' Secondary School. In the Protectorate the training of women was generally welcomed by the men although constant persuasion was needed to encourage fathers to send their girls to primary and secondary school. Evelyn Green from Derby was the Principal of Njaluahun Methodist Girls' Secondary School and she supervised the building of the boarding home. Sisters Celia Cotton and Mary Mawson developed the Women's Training Centre. Rev Stanley Brown became principal of the Segbwema Bible School and was a skilled linguist.

Bunumbu

On 6th September 1949, Leslie travelled by steam train from the Colony area into the Protectorate by the narrow gauge railway installed by the colonial government. He had been appointed to the Bunumbu circuit where there was a Church-sponsored Teacher Training College, a Central Boys' Boarding School and numerous village churches. He travelled by train to Bo and slept on the compound of the Protectorate Literature Bureau. He became acquainted with the refrain: "*The train for Bo no 'gree for go!*" He continued his journey by train to Segbwema where he was met by his Circuit Superintendent Rev F G Tucker, a missionary from Cornwall who was a graduate of Lincoln College, Oxford, where John Wesley had been a Fellow. They travelled with a lorry and arrived in Bunumbu Town in a tropical rainstorm.

On 12 September 1949 he arrived in Bunumbu along muddy roads in the rainy season. He was given an enthusiastic welcome by the town. He was presented with gifts of live chickens, cola nuts (*famalolei*) and country cloth which was spun and woven from locally grown cotton and coloured with natural dyes. There was also an abundance of rice, cocoa and coffee, all locally grown. On his second day in Bunumbu Leslie received a telegram from the Mission House in London asking him if he had made a will!

One of the leaders of the local Church was Mr Jambawai whose son Musa later became Secretary of the Conference of the Methodist Church Sierra Leone while his daughter Battu became a Vice President of the World Federation of Methodist and Uniting Church Women. The mission house in Bunumbu was in need of repair and when the monsoon rains were in full spate he marked the spots where the roof was leaking, with chalk on the floor, so that the holes in the thatch roof could be repaired. There were 26 circles in the floor by the time morning came.

Leslie took this all in his stride and no doubt the situation was ameliorated by the warmth of the welcome and by the fact that the compound around the house contained bright flowers such as hibiscus, bougainvillea and pride of Barbados and flame trees with fiery red flowers and black seed pods which looked like boomerangs. The whitewashed stones which outlined the red laterite clay path to the house seemed to add their own welcome to the new resident. There were numerous kinds of fruit trees such as mango, banana, papaya, orange, grapefruit, lemon and lime as well as pineapple bushes and groundnuts. Leslie did not know that pineapples grew as plants or bananas grew on trees. One evening when returning to the mission house he found three enterprising little boys from his Central School catechism class. They sold him bananas from his own garden! No one had yet told him that you should eat bananas when they are green. Irish potatoes would not grow in the heat and humidity, no matter how much he tried nor how high were the stems. He wore a pith helmet of which he was fond as it had many uses, not least in protecting the eyes before the availability of sunglasses. With pith helmet and leather mosquito boots he may have looked like someone in the colonial service but his attitude was far removed from European paternalism. From reading the gospels, he knew that all human beings are created in the image of God and are equally loved by God. He knew that Christ died on the cross for each human being as equally valuable. He knew that: "God is no respecter of persons" (Romans 2:11). He did not believe in a limited atonement and he knew Charles Wesley's hymn: "For all, for all, my Saviour died, for all my Lord was crucified." He loved to preach about the cross and what William Arthur called: "the ever-speaking blood of Jesus."

Leslie quickly acclimatised. Here, instead of the four seasons of spring, summer, autumn and winter, there were the two seasons, the wet and the dry. He learned to care for oil lamps and Tilley lamps. Darkness and dawn happened with startling speed because of proximity to the equator and day and night lasted about 12 hours each. The people were mostly subsistence farmers growing rice, upland and swamp, as well as some vegetables. Meat and fish were caught or chickens were reared. Commercial transactions were effected by a mixture of cash and barter. The church offerings, especially at the harvest thanksgiving celebrations were made in kind and sold. One of the churches kept the money in a cloth placed in a hole in the mud floor underneath the communion table and there was no lock on the door. Seldom would a national policeman be seen in the villages. Villages were self-policed through a system of village taboos and the close knit extended family structures.

Methodist missionaries, unlike some others, lived simply. In the village they had no electricity or running water and their furniture was home-made. Their homes were open. Their financial stipend was less than they would have received had they stayed in their own country. It is true that most of them had a means of transport but this was as much for the benefit of the community as for the work of the church. They followed a lifestyle which aimed to be incarnational and contextual and in keeping with their surroundings. On more than one occasion Leslie used his vehicle to help pregnant mothers get to hospital in time. The first time such help was required, soon after he arrived in Bunumbu, was for the birth of twins. One twin was born in a house in the town but the second was delayed. He was called upon by the women to take the distressed mother to the Wesley Guild hospital in Segbwema. When the lady with her baby was being helped into the Bedford van, some men, who had been keeping the required discreet distance from the maternity proceedings, arrived and one of them identified himself as the father. He sat on the mudguard for the journey. The journey of 17 miles was bumpy on laterite dirt roads. The missionary maternity sister explained later that the bumpy journey was beneficial and the second twin was quickly born. There were superstitions about twins and some communities were less than welcoming of the second child to be born. The mission of Christ gave

Chief's compound Bunumbu 1928

Union College Bunumbu 1928

equal dignity to all human beings because all are created in the image of God.

Although Bunumbu was a small rural community it was none the less an important centre for the Methodist Church. The Methodist Church began a mission station there in 1921. Segbwema had seen Methodist work spread in 1908 by Rev James Walton followed later by Rev Henry N Medd. In Bunumbu, from 1923 until the late 1940s the Methodist Church operated a Catechist Training School which later incorporated a Teacher Training Institution staffed by Methodist missionaries including Rev Kenneth Crosby, Rev L W Juby, Rev W T Harris, Rev Stanley Brown and Rev Eric Wright. Four of these wrote books in connection with the Mende. Kenneth Crosby was from Wales where they seem to sing their language. Perhaps this helped him with the tonal Mende language and he wrote *A study of the Mende language* which was his PhD thesis. Tom Harris wrote papers and *Springs of Mende Belief and Conduct* (with Canon Harry Sawyerr). Eric Wright wrote *Behind the Lion Mountains*. Stanley Brown wrote several booklets in Mende including *A Mende Primer* and an article on *Nomoli*.

The Methodist Teachers College had originally started in Tikonko in the Southern Province where the Principal was Rev W E A Pratt. As the work among the Mende began to grow in the Eastern Province, the Teachers College was transferred to Bunumbu and would later, in 1933, become Union College Bunumbu. Rev Kenneth Crosby was the first Principal and Dr John Karefa-Smart was one of the early lecturers. The College was called Union College because in 1933 the Methodists were joined by the United Brethren and the Church Missionary Society in the joint sponsorship of the project. Dr Crosby also helped to found the Bunumbu Press which began in a bedroom of the No.2 mission bungalow. Kenneth Crosby was popular throughout the region as his language skills enabled him to draw alongside people. Several babies were given the Christian name 'Kenneth' including a future Paramount Chief, Kenneth S L Kangoma and a future secondary school Principal, Kenneth Paul Ganna Conteh. Dr Crosby loved the Mende language and contributed to its orthography and to the translation of the Bible. He wrote of the Mende language: "I was brought up on the classics and had been taught that classical Greek was the most perfect instrument of speech ever devised. I accepted this, of course, unthinkingly and believed it implicitly until I met the Mende language. But then I began to think differently. I marvelled at its incredible beauty, its wonderful cadences, its skilful nuances and the deeper I went the more I learned to wonder."

In 1946 the Catechist Training School had moved to Njaluahun, near Segbwema. The premises at Bunumbu had become the site of Union Teachers' College which was a Church and Government collaboration. It is unclear why the training of catechists moved from Bunumbu. The initial purpose of a training college for mission teachers included training in the teaching of the bible. Alongside the training of teachers was a programme for the training of Mende-speaking catechists. It seemed a sensible and integrated arrangement. It may be that with Government involvement and a change in the national education policy which demanded higher standards in schools and colleges, it was felt that the training in the vernacular of catechists required a dedicated site where there would be less distractions and more control. The buildings on the Bunumbu campus with the two mission houses were retained by the College and new manses were built at Bunumbu and Bandajuma Yawei. Leslie was chaplain to the College. Rev Ewart Prickett was an enthusiastic scholar and lecturer. Generations of teachers were trained and served the nation well in schools and churches. The first Mende Methodist ministers were trained here before going on to Fourah Bay College. They were Daniel D. Tucker, Philip F. Jibao and Samuel M. Musa. Several of the first Africans to become Secondary School principals studied here including K P G Conteh, T M Tengbeh and S G Baihinga. A M Lahai was trained at Njala.

Leslie was committed to evangelism and the saving of souls yet he was keen to promote education for life, both in English and in the vernacular languages. The Christian gospel is holistic. The spiritual gospel is accompanied by the social development of people after the pattern of Jesus who came preaching and fed the hungry, healed the sick and taught that we should love God with our mind. All of this was in the succession of the first official Wesleyan missionary in Africa, Rev George Warren, who wrote on his way to Freetown in 1811: "I want to teach them how to read and write and how to be happy after death." The Kingdom of God is not coterminous with the church but is larger than it and involves all of human life in this present physical world as well as in the spiritual world to come. The gospel is the good news of the Kingdom of God.

Leslie was trained in the management of schools by F G Tucker. Travelling was by foot along forest paths between small villages and hamlets. He would appear, wearing his pith helmet, equipped with his camp bed and mosquito net, dependent on the hospitality of the people. He found that sleeping in a mud house with palm thatch roof was cooler than a house with tin roof. He preached the gospel at every opportunity in villages and in rice farms, accompanied by catechists or teachers who assisted in translation. Churches were being built at a great rate. A policy was developed encouraging local congregations to build their church to roof height with the Mission providing the roofing timbers, nails and thatch or corrugated iron. Each church building, no matter how basic, had a bell. It was either a suspended metal rim of a lorry wheel or a metal sleeper from the railway which was struck with a large bolt, iron rod or starting handle. It was a most effective means of calling the farmers from their fields.

It took Leslie a long time to get used to the meat or fish stew made with cassava leaf or sweet potato leaf cooked in palm oil and with chilli peppers. He learned not to ask what the meat was until after he had eaten. As well as river fish, exotic meats were eaten such as monkey, 'cutting grass' (cane rat), porcupine, duika, boa, goat, lamb and chicken. He would walk through, or sometimes be carried through leech-infested swamps. All of this was new to him. Monkeys, chameleons and the noisy yellow weaver birds, building their nests in the shape of a suspended inverted sock, were an amazing novelty. Crocodiles, snakes, scorpions and the occasional five feet long monitor lizard were more dangerous novelties. A large black mamba caused a disturbance in the compound one day and was helpfully shot by a Lebanese neighbour. The snake was eaten. There were two Lebanese trading families in the town, the John family and the Saad family. Their religion was Orthodox Christian yet they, like many Lebanese, greatly helped the Methodist Mission.

Diseases which were becoming rare in Europe were still rife including polio, yaws and tuberculosis. An extension clinic from the Methodist Mission Hospital at Segbwema had been built in Bunumbu and was combating these and other illnesses.

For the first time Leslie encountered polygamy or met witch doctors and native healers. The traditional healers were a mixed blessing. On the positive side, some of them were experts in herbalist treatments where modern facilities were non-existent or unaffordable. Sometimes Leslie would enter a village and find a person tied in chains because of mental illness which issued in violence. Confronted with this new world, Leslie never suffered from culture shock. He understood that the incarnation of Christ was the greatest cross-cultural move and that his own missionary calling was derived from that event. God is a missionary God and wherever God would place him, there would be his home. He never doubted his missionary calling. The Christians in Bunumbu taught him to sing in Mende: "Trust and obey, for there's no other way to be happy in Jesus" and he believed it to be true.

In this fresh encounter between the Christian faith and the old religions of Africa, the practice of polygamy (polygyny) exercised his mind. The Koran allowed four wives. Indigenous customs had no such limit. Leslie asked the right questions. Does it matter? Is it a sin? Does it deny the gospel? Upon reflection on the New Testament the answer to all of these questions was 'yes'. The equality of one man and one woman was given in creation and the teaching of Christ was that marriage was a covenant between two equal parties, a man and a woman. However the strict tradition of all churches created problems in this matter. Sometimes catechists fell foul of this prohibition and lost their jobs. A polygamous man could not be baptised but his first wife could receive baptism and Holy Communion. For the polygamous husband to be a church member he had to keep the first wife and abandon the others. This often caused social upheaval, especially for older women, some of whom were left destitute. Many chiefs and elders were polygamous and their place of respect was undermined by the church when their wives could receive the sacraments of the church but they could not, even though they were converted. The policy of the churches modified in later years when a polygamous man was allowed to become a catechumen or seeker and progress to become a member 'on trial' but not a full member, even if he had come to faith and been saved. No legislation was passed on the matter because monogamy was gradually becoming the norm. Eventually in some churches polygamous men who were converted became full members upon a promise that they would acquire no more wives and that they would teach their children the importance of monogamy. At times there was debate about the matter of dowry which some understood to be a bride price and which others regarded as means of social contract. It was a custom that women sat separately in church, from the men.

Membership of 'secret' initiation societies was another vexed issue where all Mende men belonged to the Poro Society and all Mende women belonged to the Sande or Bundu Society. Initiation societies form a social and cultural system of education and schooling. They include civil and religious functions. The hold of the Poro and Sande societies is pervasive. When the *poro* devil processes through the village, any non-initiates, including missionaries, have to consent to being locked in their room with the wooden shutters closed and their lanterns doused, lest they break a taboo and view the devil and incur enforced initiation. Among the Kissy and Kono people, the hold of secret societies, while pervasive, appeared to be less intense. Missionaries tended to be divided on such issues, with some being confrontational and others, in common with most of their members, tending towards assimilation. Another cultural issue which perplexed the missionaries was the physical punishment of children or wives and it was always difficult to know when to intervene.

These were exciting times. Membership of the church was growing, the gospel was spreading, new churches were planted and many were being baptised. At first the baptisms were mainly of adult believers who were the first generation Christians. Baptisms would sometimes take place by immersion in the river, especially where there was no church building. In later times more infants were baptised. A maternity clinic was opened as an extension of the Methodist Mission Hospital at Segbwema and the infant mortality rate of 60% was reduced. The rapid spread of Christianity was due to different reasons. The gospel message was welcomed as good news of love and hope and triumph over the fear of the spirit world. There was also the desire of provincial chiefs and their peoples to have access to the new resources that were becoming readily available through the missions. These included schools, literacy programmes, clinics and hospitals.

After a matter of months at Bunumbu, Leslie received a telegram from London and was directed to proceed temporarily to The Gambia where the only two ministers had died. After one year he would return to Bunumbu Circuit and reside at Bandajuma Yawei only to be temporarily transferred to Kailahun for five months to replace Rev L Clarke who was on furlough.

While at Bandajuma Yawei, with the help of catechists and trainee teachers, he was part of the pioneer outreach, on foot, through forests and over the Gori hills to the Chiefdom town of Sandaru in the Penguia Chiefdom adjacent to the country of Guinea. These forest treks required energy and a constant lookout for leopards or snakes.

Sometimes they would trek from Manowa junction up to Sandaru, preaching and baptising as they went. Often the chief allowed the preaching to take place in the *barrie* which was the open-sided community centre or court. Later in this remote area five schools, a mission house and maternity clinic were built. The first resident ministers were Revs Sidney Groves and Roger Smith whose wives were medically trained; Mary Groves was a doctor and Glenys Smith was a nursing sister. Some of these villages had waited a long time for someone to plant the seeds of the gospel. Leslie remembers the special thrill as he arrived in a village, the first white person to do so, and shared the Christian gospel for the first time. Little children held his hands, perhaps four or five children noisily holding each hand as he walked into the village. One child suggested that he whitened his face every morning. Another child once explained to the rest in the Mende language that the missionary was white because he had no blood in him, only water.

In the Penguia area, where three tribal groups met, Mende, Kono and Kissy, the people had not embraced the Islamic faith. The spirit world was very real and feared. Sometimes the primal religions were called 'animist,' 'polytheist,' 'pagan,' or improperly 'ancestor worship.' Among the Mende, Kissy and Kono people there was belief in a supreme being named *Ngewo, Hala Melekah* and *Yatah,* respectively. Such a supreme being was remote and religious practices centred upon other spiritual beings both good and malevolent, as well as the ancestral spirits. Pagan animism held people in fear of evil spirits and witchcraft. Charms and 'fear fetishes' were worn and sacrifices offered for protection. These charms ('medicines') were dispensed with when a person embraced the liberating gospel message which declared: "Fear not." The Trinitarian gospel message proclaimed: God as Father who loves all whom he has made; God the Son by whose self-sacrifice on the cross all may be forgiven and no other sacrifice is ever required; God the Holy Spirit who is greater than any fearsome evil spirit or demon. To know God as the Father creating us, the Son redeeming us and the Spirit indwelling us, is eternal life. In addition, the fear of death is removed because Christ our Saviour has conquered death by his resurrection from the dead. This liberating gospel was welcome news. Leslie commented: "It was wonderful to see some school boys and some student teachers being delivered from the paralysis of limbs and throat as they prayed a prayer of confession and sought the power of Jesus who was more powerful than the demons or 'Jinni' which bound them."

This gospel message was spread by faithful catechists and teachers around the villages and it gained widespread acceptance. Many were converted, renounced pagan practices and rejoiced in the knowledge of God as 'Father.' The employment, training and deployment of catechists formed a major evangelistic strategy in the villages. New converts were trained as catechumens or seekers before baptism after which they were recorded as members 'on trial.' To become a Full Member one had to become literate and recite some passages such as the Lord's Prayer, the Ten Commandments and the Apostles' Creed. The Penguia area produced celebrated Methodist ministers like Rev Francis Nabieu, Rev Karimu Mbawa, Rev Dr Sahr Yambasu, Rev Sahr Aruna and Rev Sahr Wubembe as well as many teachers for mission schools.

Leslie's administrative gifts were quickly being recognised and he was soon appointed as Secretary of the Mende Area Council and as Assistant Synod Secretary for the Sierra Leone District. Later, with the support of Rev T A Beetham at the Mission House in London, he became a founder member of the Islam in Africa project led by Lamin Sanneh, John Crossley and John Loum, doing a good work for the Kingdom of God.

Christian witness to Muslims was more by private conversation rather than public confrontation although sometimes the latter was necessary. In official national events Muslims and Christians would be invited to offer public prayers. This took place in two consecutive parts. It was not possible to pretend that all religions were the same when plainly they are not. So the prayers were said in series rather than in parallel. One religion would lead in its prayers and then step aside for the other religion to lead in prayer. The Muslims would usually pray first in Arabic, followed by the Christians. There was an occasion when travelling to conduct worship, he stopped his car in response to a distressed man's appeal to get his pregnant wife to hospital in time. There was no public transport available. Leslie acted as 'the good Samaritan' and brought them to hospital. Later the Muslim man stopped him, thanked him for his help and told him that he had named the new-born child: 'Mohammed Wallace.'

While at Bandajuma Yawei Leslie became conscious that many men were attracted to the diamond mining area further north in the Kono District and were being lost to the church. Later in 1970 he promoted joint work with the United Methodist Church (former EUB) in this area and created structures for the Koidu Joint Parish as an outreach strategy for mission and evangelism in the diamond mining area of Kono.

CHAPTER 3

THE GAMBIA

Leslie had long since abandoned himself to Divine providence. So in November 1949, in accordance with the instructions in a telegram, he packed 66 lbs. of luggage and proceeded to Freetown because he was being sent to Bathurst, Gambia, where the only two Gambian Methodist ministers, Rev Mr McLean and Rev Mr Cole had died within a month of each other. The missionary Chairman, Rev Mr Summerfield, had proceeded to the United Kingdom on leave, prior to retirement. It was the first time Leslie had flown in an aeroplane. It was a small freight plane that had been used in wartime and had only two passenger seats. During the flight his fellow passenger became agitated and began making the sign of the cross many times. Upon enquiry he showed Leslie that one of the two engines was leaking oil which was splashing against his window. The pilot was informed so he flew the plane tilted to the one side to conserve oil, before landing safely in Bathurst on a makeshift runway of metal strips on the sand. There was a welcome party of Methodist stewards in black suits and striped trousers. Leslie was dressed in shorts with pith helmet and walked past them until later he was told that they were there to meet him. The date was 10 November 1949.

The church office was opposite Methodist Boys' High School and it was here he slept on a camp bed while accommodation was prepared for him. In the church were several plaques in memory of deceased missionaries, some of whom died within their first year. It was a sober thought. With the car placed at his disposal, a new tradition began. It was the custom at church funerals for the corpse to be carried the two miles from Bathurst to the graveyard by means of a handcart or carriage as the mourners sang Christian hymns. A child of one of the

Gambia Youth Group 1950

church members died and the family could not afford the cost of the carriage. Leslie offered to transport the family in the mission car to the burial ground with the little white coffin placed across the knees of the parents in the back seat. In the newspaper next day was the headline: "Minister rushes dead to graveyard" reporting on this first use of motorised transport for a funeral. Before long it was not only the mission car but others which were conveying people and corpses from Bathurst to the cemetery.

It was surely a sign of the maturity of the man that he was chosen to act as the Secretary of The Gambia District so soon in his ministry and while still on probation. The experience was not wasted on him. It was his practice to visit the people in their homes, praying with them and administering the Lord's Supper to those unable to come to church. Some of the homes were poor and infested and there was a perceived need for the church to promote low-cost housing schemes. The church ran programmes for the youth and supported agricultural schemes. The agenda of Christian mission is large. Mission includes spirituality, evangelism and church growth, justice and service, development and economic empowerment. Mission is sharing the life that Jesus has and doing the things that Jesus did. It is living life in the light of Providence.

Christian mission seeks transformation of communities as well as converts.

Such a full surrender to Christ was re-iterated in the words of the Covenant service which he conducted in Bathurst on the first Sunday of 1950:

I am no longer my own, but Yours.

Put me to what You will, rank me with whom You will;

Put me to doing, put me to suffering;

Let me be employed for You or laid aside for You,

Exalted for You or brought low for You;

Let me be full, let me be empty,

Let me have all things, let me have nothing;

I freely and wholeheartedly yield all things to Your pleasure and disposal.

And now, glorious and blessed God, Father, Son and Holy Spirit, You are mine and I am Yours.

So be it.

And the covenant now made on earth, let it be ratified in heaven. Amen.

Leslie was still a probationer minister and was expected to pursue studies for ordination at this time. His college friend David Turtle, who later served as a missionary in Burma, sent by post some study books in a shoebox. Leslie received them one year later after they had been sent to Bunumbu in Sierra Leone and then forwarded to Bathurst, Gambia. Having said this, the British Government was rightly proud of the reliability of its postal system throughout the Empire.

Leslie commented:

"In The Gambia (1949-1950) the Methodists and other churches ministered to the strongly Muslim community through excellent mission schools, both primary and secondary. There were several missionary teachers from the UK who were also fully accredited local preachers. These together with Gambian colleagues, conducted services in churches on the island of St Mary, on the mainland and up-river. At one mission station 175 miles inland at George Town on McCarthy Island, 95% of the enrolled children were Muslim. Mr Coker was head teacher, local preacher and pastor who travelled down river by boat to

Synod once per year. Synod requested a report on the sanitary conditions of the mission house as Mr Coker and other teachers had been ill. On a visit I noted that the drinking water was drawn from the same part of the river as the 'night soil' bucket contents were deposited. The drinking water had not been boiled, just filtered. This practice was corrected and the health of the teachers improved."

Rev G L Frost a retired chaplain to the British forces arrived to act as District Chairman. Upon the arrival of Rev John Stanfield as missionary, Leslie was able to return to Sierra Leone. This experience of life in another West African country would help him later when he became Chair of the West African Methodist Council.

CHAPTER 4

ORDINATION IN IRELAND AND RETURN TO THE KAILAHUN DISTRICT

Samuel Leslie Wallace was ordained at the Irish Conference in the Grosvenor Hall, Belfast, in June 1951 in the presence of Rev Dr Edwin Sangster (British President) and Rev W J Wesley Roddie (Irish President). Dr Sangster preached on the text from Revelation 17:14: "Because he is Lord of lords and King of kings - and with him will be his called, and chosen and faithful followers." He told the ordinands who were called and chosen and faithful, to take their wages from God. Sometimes they would be paid with the praises of people but their true wages were Christ's approval and his promise of blessing. He was ordained with colleagues including Wilfred Agnew, Sydney Callaghan, Brian Dougall, Charles Eyre, George Ferguson, Joe McCrory, Jim McEvoy, Cecil Newell, Tom Sawyer and Robin Smith.

He returned to Sierra Leone that same year and was appointed to the east of the country to superintend the large Kailahun Circuit for the next five years 1951-1956. The District catechist was Pa JT Rogers and they became friends for many years. J T Rogers was fluent in Mende, Kissy and English. While they were approaching the town, they heard the sound of gunshots. Pa Rogers explained that the guns must be announcing the arrival of the District Commissioner, representing the Government. Leslie soon realised that the gunfire was to welcome him to the town and explained that they were representatives of the King of kings! A little boy named Joseph Bockarie who was the nephew of Pa Rogers. liked to accompany his uncle and Leslie on trek around the villages and carry the Mende Hymn book and the Gospel of St Luke. The whole Bible had not yet been translated. Later that young man committed his life to Christ at a Boys' Brigade Service in Kailahun. Much later he would be employed in the City of Dublin, Ireland, as a civil engineer and serve as Circuit Steward of the Dublin Methodist Central Mission and be a representative at the Irish Methodist Conference.

For the next five years in the widespread Kailahun Circuit, churches grew in Mende and Kissy areas and because the gospel knows no boundaries, evangelism over-spilled into Liberia. This was the territory travelled by Graham Greene and graphically described in his book *African Creeks I've been up.* With Pa Rogers, Leslie was responsible for evangelism, church planting, primary school management and the plan for a Methodist Secondary School. In his evangelistic work, he followed the routine of a seven day trek from Kailahun to the villages and back to Kailahun. He had the use of an Austin A40 country van but mostly trekking was by foot. Sometimes he would travel by dug-out canoe at Dodo Kotuma in the direction of Sandaru, trespassing into Guinea until the border guards forcibly prevented this shortcut.

On one evening when he was preaching in the open air, the kerosene of his hurricane lantern ran out and he had yet to walk home. Some children kindly went out and collected the fireflies which were flickering brightly in the night. They captured them in a glass jar with a lid to

Taken with Rev Dr Edwin Sangster at Irish Methodist Conference 1951.
Back row L-R: Charles Eyre; George Ferguson; Wilfred Agnew; Brian Dougall; Sydney Callaghan; Cecil Newell; Robin Smith. Front row L-R: T Sawyer; Leslie Wallace; Dr W E Sangster (British President); J Wesley Roddie (Irish President); Joe McCrory; Jim McEvoy.

serve as a flashlight for the preacher to navigate his way home along the bush path. Their kindly scheme did not work well because the fireflies shine most brightly when they are free, rather like the birds which sing more sweetly when they are uncaged. He arrived home to the mission house and heard the chain rattle on the stand for the oil lamp. A large snake escaped into his bedroom. It was a spitting cobra and he would not sleep until he dispatched it with a machete. So ferocious was the blow that the damage to the wooden floor of the mission remained for years.

Church planting continued. The gospel of the Lord Jesus Christ is the grand message which every human being was created with a longing to hear. The message was received and believed by many. These in turn proceeded to plant new churches. The stories of Jesus were being shared by school children or traders so that even unchurched people were able to sing: "*Wa Yesu gama sange*" ("Come to Jesus now") or recite the Lord's Prayer, the Ten Commandments and even the Beatitudes in their own languages. The children were natural dramatists. They could re-enact any Bible story when it was told to them only once. At Easter the plain churches built of mud and thatch were transformed by plaited palm branches dotted with red hibiscus flowers. Children and adults joyfully re-enacted, with dancing, the Palm Sunday procession of our Lord into Jerusalem in the week that he was crucified. The Christmas story was likewise an opportunity for spontaneous unscripted drama celebrating the birth of Jesus. Joyful Christmases in sweltering heat were celebrated without any trinkets but with palm branches, dance, drama and faith. Sometimes churches would prepare a feast of rice and stew and meat or fish to which the whole village was invited.

At Christmas time there is a meteorological phenomenon when the climate changes for about three weeks with the arrival of the dry dusty harmattan wind blowing from the Sahara desert to the north. Normal temperature during the year is around 30 degrees C (86 degrees F) and relative humidity averages 80% over the year. When the harmattan comes, the air becomes dry, people get colds and cracked lips and there is a light covering of red dust everywhere. Some welcome the harmattan, most do not.

It was the practice, when leading worship, to recite the verse of the hymn before it was sung and then halt the singing and do the same for successive verses so that those who were illiterate could sing along. Plainly, literacy and Bible translation were vital to the spread of the gospel. It was estimated that the rate of illiteracy in the Protectorate was 86%. Classes were organised for those who had no opportunity of attending primary school. They were taught in their mother tongue using the novel adult literacy method practised in India by Dr Frank Laubach and adapted for Sierra Leone by Rev R A Johnston. It spread with the 'each one teach one' strategy. Leslie had a wireless which he shared with a local trader from time to time. People could listen to national broadcasts as well as the BBC World Service which was an aid to learning English. As village church work grew the children were catered for in new primary schools. The circuit minister, as school manager, was responsible for the opening of primary schools. He negotiated with the Chiefs for land. He arranged for the supply of building materials for the construction of class rooms, teachers' houses, deep-pit latrines and wells for water supply. Classroom furniture also had to be provided when the nearest suitable tree was felled and carpenters made the benches, desks, tables, chairs and cupboards. The purchase and provision of reading books, exercise books, slates, chalk, pencils, rubbers and rulers were also the responsibility of the school manager. A historic moment occurred when the site for a future Kailahun Methodist Secondary School was acquired by Leslie in negotiations with the Paramount Chief.

His successor in Kailahun was Rev Ken Nicholson who had married Marion Copithorne, a university graduate from Ireland. Ken gave oversight to the building of the school and Marion became the first Principal of Kailahun Methodist Secondary School which would become a leading educational institution. The resident District Commissioner was a young man from Dublin whose father was a bishop. D.C. Hughes was most helpful especially in the area of school expansion. Leslie was happy to co-operate with the colonial power where the higher values of the Kingdom of God were concerned. He was however more interested in spreading the life-transforming good news of Christianity rather than in promoting a Christendom that could be plotted on a map.

Travel was challenging along unformed roads which took their toll on the leaf springs of a Landrover. Accidents happened, often on flimsy wooden bridges over ravines. He remembers stretching his first-aid training to repair the partially severed ear of a survivor. When called to visit Freetown he would drive from Kailahun and leave his vehicle at Pendembu which was the end or beginning of the railway line. He recalls a new train being acquired for the line and it was called an Express Train which was publicised as being able to complete the journey from Freetown to Pendembu in one day. Sometimes it did. One day when the train was de-railed in a forested area an elderly grandmother appeared after several hours in the hot sun with a bucket of water which she would only give to the babies first. Later her granddaughter appeared with a bucket of water which was for adults, but not for him because a coconut was being brought for him, complete with drinking hole in it. No doubt Leslie told that story as an introduction to a sermon of the Good Samaritan and often told it in Ireland to children in schools or at Junior Missionary Association services.

It was at this time that Bible translation was making progress, encouraged by the Mende Area Council. In 1872 German missionaries had begun translation of the Bible into Mende. The work was incomplete but they left their manuscripts and suggestions for orthography with the Methodist Church. Rev Kenneth Crosby furthered the work with others. In the 1950s Rev J R S Law was set apart to standardise the work of orthography and oversee the translation of the Bible into Mende. He worked under the auspices of the Methodist Church Mende Area Council. J R S Law selected Jojoima as the base for his work, believing that the pure deep Mende was spoken in this area notwithstanding the two strands of the language, Koh Mende and Kpaa Mende. The task was gigantic and required a collaborative approach. Mr S A Junisa, who was a lecturer in Union College, was a member of the Mende Area Council. He and the members received portions of the scriptures to be tested at village level using the catechists. A portion of the Bible would be translated and typed using carbon paper to make five copies. The translations were judged at the bar of village opinion often causing hilarity as words were misunderstood or wrongly used. Pa Kpanga Edwards of the Literature Bureau in Bo was another translator. Manuscripts were sent off to the Bible Society in London who forwarded them to the USA to check the orthography.

The Mende New Testament was completed in 1956 and the whole Bible in 1959. When the final manuscript was complete, Pa Law carried the precious document in his suitcase on board ship to Liverpool. It was the only copy. Leslie was travelling on the same ship to go on furlough in Ireland. He offered to help carry the suitcase but he was not allowed. He asked in vain to see the manuscript. Pa Law slept with it under his bunk bed on board ship and never let it out of his sight. From the ship he travelled directly to London and handed over the unique manuscript.

At the end of five years in Kailahun, Rev W.T. Harris visited Leslie and on behalf of the United Christian Council and the Synod, he asked him to transfer to Bo to manage the Provincial Literature Bureau and Bunumbu Printing Press and promote literacy programmes for the nation.

Leslie's reputation for evangelical zeal and school development was never forgotten in Kailahun. When he returned in later years to preside at the opening of a new church in the town, he was greeted by the Paramount Chief and head teacher Kenneth S L Kangoma with Dr Sama Banya and the minister Rev Richard Thompson. They dressed him in African robes as honorary Chief and he was carried around the town in a hammock in joyful dance. He looked uncomfortable as his porters danced and the hammock swayed, yet he maintained a dignified smile dispensing royal waves to enthusiastic crowds.

Leslie moved to Bo in 1956 and became Director of the United Christian Council Literature Bureau and Bunumbu Printing Press. He succeeded Rev R A Johnston who returned to circuit in England. He was also appointed Assistant Secretary of the West African Conference and was the Methodist Missionary Society's representative in Sierra Leone at a time when there were numerous missionaries in the country serving in medical, educational, administrative and pastoral appointments.

CHAPTER 5

MARRIAGE IN IRELAND AND RETURN TO BO

Wedding 1958

Leslie returned home to Ireland on furlough to Bangor, Northern Ireland in 1958. On a previous leave in 1956 he was spoken to by Mrs Jane Curry, a discerning lady with matchmaking intentions who suggested to him that he should speak again with Agnes Thompson who would go with him to Africa or to the ends of the earth. Leslie took the hint and invited Agnes for a walk around the coast to a local beauty spot called Pickie Pool. His proposal was accepted and they were engaged to be married. He then returned to Sierra Leone while Agnes went for missionary training at Selly Oak College, Birmingham, under the auspices of the Methodist Missionary Society. Two years later they were married in Mountpottinger Methodist Church, Belfast, on June 25th 1958 when the officiating ministers were Revs John Young and J Dwyer Kelly.

In 1958 Rev Leslie Wallace and Mrs Agnes Wallace arrived off the

Rev SL and Mrs Wallace

coast of Freetown and were transported from the ship by barge in the usual way. They made their way to Bo, in the centre of the country, by steam train. It was here that they lived on the compound of the Provincial Literature Bureau and the Bunumbu Printing Press. The Bunumbu Printing Press which had begun in a small way in Bunumbu in the 1920s had moved in the 1930s to Bo which was a more central location and had electricity. The Commonwealth Fund gave £25,000 for development of the Bunumbu Press Building and for staff houses. Rev Ray Johnston supervised the building work. Illiteracy was widespread in the country and the workers at the Printing Press were committed to translating and publishing literacy materials and primers in indigenous languages of Kono, Mende, Loko, Themne, Limba, Mandinka and Krio. Agnes helped in this work, educating families on the compound. Leslie recalls one Mende man in Moyamba, who by the light of an oil lamp, read a portion of the Gospel of Luke in a test for his coveted reading certificate. The man chose to read the same passage a second time aloud and exclaimed: "Sir, God's book is talking to me." It felt as if a goal had been reached. God's revealed and revealing word is always a word for today and a word for us all.

It was a great shock and sadness for Agnes and Leslie to lose the first and third pregnancies and those three children, a girl and twin boys are buried at the side of their former mission house in the Bunumbu Printing Press compound at Bo. God blessed them with a loved and loving daughter Verena who was born in the Royal Maternity Hospital in Belfast. Verena later became a midwife in the United Kingdom. She takes a keen interest in Sierra Leone and has revisited the country on several occasions. When Agnes and the baby Verena, returned to Bo a little kindergarten was started on the mission house veranda. Verena still loves Dr Seuss books and can still count in the Mende language.

The work of the United Christian Council Provincial Literature Bureau and Bunumbu Printing Press continued unabated. A new Heidelberg automatic printing machine was purchased. It was the most advanced of its type in the country. There was great excitement when the new machine arrived in the compound but it was a problem to unload it from the lorry. No crane was available. In the railway workshop were two managers who willingly came to the compound to give advice, since a train was not expected until evening. The door of the Printing Press was too small and when they discovered that the building was made of mud block and cement plaster, they demolished part of the wall. Ropes and eight crowbars and many men helped to off-load the delicate precision cargo. However when the lorry was backed against the wall, the floor of the lorry was six inches higher than the floor of the building. A tropical rainstorm was expected. From 8 a.m. to 2 p.m. they tried to unload the cargo. Much to the distress of the lorry driver Leslie asked that he deflate the tyres of his lorry and when this was done they were able to slide the load from the lorry into the building.

The Prime Minister of Sierra Leone, Dr Milton A S Margai, visited Bo in 1958 asked Leslie to come to see him. Dr Margai knew that 86% of people in the nation were illiterate. He encouraged literacy, not least among the women because, as a medical doctor he saw a problem with the practice of female circumcision and perceived literacy as providing an eventual solution to the practice within the *Sande* Society or the *Bundu* bush. He asked the Mission to prepare a National Literacy Programme, in preparation for political independence. This was adopted by the Government in time to prepare the nation for voting for Independence. One of the follow-up booklets printed by the Bunumbu Press was 'How to Vote' and as Leslie pointed out, the title was not: 'For whom to vote!'

The preparation and printing of literacy materials involved extensive labour. It included the production of literacy charts, primers for adults and children, a teachers' handbook and follow-up readers that related to the house, the village and the farm. Also produced were hymnals, books on prayer and the stories of Jesus in a series of five books in English. Hospital staff provided manuscripts for health topics and various fevers. Prime Minister Dr M A S Margai wrote the manuscript for a training manual for midwives and also a midwifery catechism. These were used for the basic training of Traditional Birth Attendants (TBAs) and were printed in Mende and Themne languages. Field officers of the Ministry of Agriculture provided the finance and information for publication on farm produce including coffee, cocoa, palm nuts and poultry keeping. There were also books on history, geography and travel as well as some biographies and fiction. Two biographies were about two famous travellers Mungo Park and John Wesley.

A monthly four page newspaper in both Mende and Themne provided new readers with reading material that was fresh and relevant. Leslie enjoyed editing these new ventures which proved massively popular (called *Semei Lokoi* in Mende and *A kera kaka Themne*). They carried reports both national and international which he garnered from the press releases of the embassies, the BBC World Service and local media. Practical articles were included to promote agriculture and market gardening and the prices of produce and diamonds were published. It was read by all strata of the community. An annual vernacular calendar introduced the new reader to days and months in line with seasons and 'moon months.'

Bible translation was the major project for the churches. The Bible Society required a reasonable number of literate people in each language before it would agree to embark upon the publication of the

New Testament or the full Bible. The Printing Press at Bo was producing individual books of the New Testament. Because of the progress in literacy the Bible Society agreed to finance the production of the whole Bible in Mende.

'New Life for All' (*Ndevu ninei numui kpele va*) was an evangelistic programme which started in Nigeria and was introduced into Sierra Leone by Rev J Sedu Mans. Revs Hanimeh Sandi, John Bockari and Frank Himsworth promoted the handbook in the Mende language. The Bunumbu Printing Press produced thousands of copies. Many people were converted to Christ through this national campaign and experienced the gracious gift of eternal life in Christ. As a result churches grew and new church leaders were trained. One of Leslie's favourite texts, "You must be born again" (John 3:7) was printed on posters in different languages. Rev David Griffiths and Sister Mary Mawson continued this New Life for All campaign in the Mende towns and villages.

The Mission House in London at that time had several international Secretaries. Three of them visited the Wallaces. They were Revs T A Beetham, Dr Philip Potter and Dr Norman Taggart. Dr Potter came to ask Leslie, on behalf of the British Methodist Church, to be the Secretary of the working group preparing for the creation of the Autonomous Methodist Church, Sierra Leone. With autonomy the Methodist church in Sierra Leone would cease to be a District accountable to the British Methodist Church. This additional work would include the drafting of a Church Constitution for the Foundation Conference.

In 1967 The church appointed Leslie as Superintendent of the Bo-Tikonko Circuit for one year. Rev Warren Bardsley, whose Irish wife Joan was a Wesley Deaconess, had arrived in Bo in 1965 with their infant son John. The two families became close friends and Warren became Superintendent of the circuit and was later made Chairman of the Provincial District. Warren, like many, regards Leslie as his mentor. He remembers how the people of Bo, inside and outside of the church, responded to the pastoral care which Leslie gave with grace and dedication. He adds: "It was an education to travel with Leslie on a long journey from Bo to Freetown. He would regale you with stories of his adventures and it seemed that at every other bend in the road he had witnessed some interesting or exciting event."

Bo choir 1971

The Bo-Tikonko Circuit included numerous village churches as well as the larger St Augustine's Church in Bo. There was also a church in the compound of the Provincial Literature Bureau. Later, after the rebel war this church was re-built and called 'The Rev S L Wallace Memorial Methodist Church.' On seeing the word 'Memorial' Leslie made the wry comment that he was not yet dead! The work of the Literature Bureau was carried on by Violet Martin, Pa Kpanga Edwards and Mr Joe Tucker until the return of Rev Ray and Mrs Dorothy Johnston from England in 1966.

The lack of industrial development and investment and the consequent mass unemployment was a cause of concern and frustration. Leslie wrote: "We must provide the facilities for people to help themselves nationally." The unregulated international arms trade was another cause of concern and he commented: "When the great western powers turn their tanks and missiles into ploughshares, then God's gospel, which we share, will be seen as genuine and meaningful."

The arrival in Tikonko of Rev Dwin Capstick and his wife Ruth heralded a new development in mission. Dwin was an English Methodist minister with a farming background. He worked in the swamps with local subsistence farmers and devised, with them, improved methods of rice production. As a result the influential Tikonko Agricultural Extension Project (TAEP) was created which was of widespread benefit

51

to rice farming in the country and with the help of Njala University College, introduced new brands of swamp rice that gave increased yields and allowed two or three crops per season. The church had long been distressed by the fact that Sierra Leone used to export rice and was now importing rice.

Dwin Capstick was a remarkable minister who was knowledgeable and filled with the compassion of Christ. He was able to 'think outside the box' regarding Christian mission. In all of this work Dwin was ably supported by his wife Ruth. They did much good. Paramount Chief M K Jigba later said that besides the preaching of the gospel, the TAEC was the best thing that had happened to the Chiefdom.

Looking back on the twelve years in Bo, as Director of the Provincial Literature Bureau and the Bunumbu Printing Press, Leslie wrote:

> "The twelve years of service in adult literacy work were very fulfilling as was the expansion of the primary and secondary school programme at village level. One felt that the people, old and young, were being delivered from the bondage of illiteracy. They now had the opportunity to be independent of other people for communication with members of their family at a distance and of learning about matters relating to farming and prices and produce. They could read 'God's book.' "

CHAPTER 6

INDEPENDENCE FOR SIERRA LEONE 1961

Meeting Her Majesty Queen Elizabeth II in Bo, 1961 at the Prime Minister's Reception.

The whole country was preparing to celebrate the country's Independence. Special literature was produced at the Press. A jamboree was held in the Bo Showgrounds. In Freetown, the Prime Minister, Sir Milton Margai led the celebrations at Brookfields Stadium at which Her Majesty the Queen was represented by the Duke and Duchess of Kent. The country had a new national anthem, a new national flag and the Governor became the Governor General. The transition to Independence was peaceful and the celebrations went off well with the whole nation in party mood. Security concerns centred on a campaign of sabotage by the opposition All People's Congress Party

(APC) whose leaders Siaka Stevens and Wallace Johnston, with other Party members had been arrested a short time before and were released when the ceremonies were over. Dr Siaka Stevens would later become Prime Minister and President of the Republic of Sierra Leone and he and Leslie would share many strategic discussions both in public and in private.

Later that year Leslie met Her Majesty the Queen while she was on a State visit to the newly independent nation. He was included in the welcome group at Bo for Her Majesty and the Duke of Edinburgh. Her Majesty the Queen conversed with Leslie about the work of the church and was interested in the literacy project. The next day at Kenema Agricultural Show, Leslie was again present for the visit of Her Majesty and the Duke who visited the marquee set up by the United Christian Council Provincial Literature Bureau. When the Minister of Agriculture introduced him to the Queen she explained that they had already met in Bo. She picked up two of the books produced for the literacy programme: *Puu Yia Gaa Bukui* and *Bi Loi Mahugbe Lei* ('Caring for your child.') When the word spread that the Queen had been interested in these two books, the Press had to print an extra 10,000 of each!

Presentation of the first copy of the New Testament in Mende, 1956. L-R: Rev W R E Clark; Rev Dr W E A Pratt; Lady Dorman; Sir Maurice Dorman; Rev Dr C Renner, Rev S L Wallace.

The Governor General, Sir Maurice Dorman, was appreciative of the work of the churches and Leslie recalls his impressive speech at State House on the occasion of the presentation of the first copy of the New Testament in the Mende language. Sir Maurice recounted the positive history and influence of the Holy Bible on human development and how it provided the basis of the legal systems of most of the nations of the world.

Two years later a similar ceremony took place at State House for the presentation of the first full Mende Bible to Sir Milton Margai. Accompanied by Rev J R S Law and others who worked on the translation project, they heard Sir Milton give testimony to the power of the Bible. He explained that when he was a medical student in London and feeling lonely one afternoon he walked past the Bible Society Headquarters. He asked for a copy of the Bible in Mende. After a search he was told that there was no such book printed yet but he was given a free copy of the Gospel of Luke in the Mende language. Dr Margai read it all that evening and before going to sleep offered prayer that one day the whole Bible would be available in his mother tongue. When the Prime Minister had finished his memorable speech, he then kissed the copy of the Bible. That same copy was given to the Sierra Leone National Museum.

The year 1961 saw many expatriates leave the newly independent nation. Possibly their work was finished or some may have felt uncertainty about the future of the new nation. A church member asked Leslie if he also would be leaving. He would not be deterred from his unrelenting commitment to the work of the Kingdom of God and he carried on his work for the church and the country without hesitation or deviation. He was well able to sing, in several languages, the hymn:

> "Crowns and thrones may perish,
> Kingdoms rise and wane;
> But the Church of Jesus
> Constant shall remain."

CHAPTER 7

METHODIST CHURCH AUTONOMY

On 21st January 1967, the Foundation Conference of the Methodist Church, Sierra Leone was held in Wesley Church, Trelawney Street (now Lamina Sankoh Street), Freetown. The first President of Conference was the greatly beloved Rev Dr W E Akinumi Pratt, OBE, MA. The first Vice-President of Conference was Mr Ephraim J Robinson JP, CH, who was a retired teacher and a local preacher. The Secretary of Conference was Leslie.

Special prayer meetings were held in preparation for the Conference. The prayer was that God would launch the Methodist Church on a new future of service for the Kingdom of the Lord Jesus Christ and that there would be spiritual transformation in the nation. The Rev Dr Frederick Greeves, Ex-President of the British Conference was present to inaugurate the Conference. Also present from Britain were the Vice-President Mr Albert F Bayley and Rev Hugh Thomas and Miss Betty Hares. These official representatives together with Sierra Leonean members appointed by the Synod, signed the Deed of Foundation thus constituting The Conference of the Methodist Church, Sierra Leone.

It seemed as if the whole of Freetown was in celebration mood for Methodist Autonomy. There were flags and bunting around the churches. There were marches of witness with singing and dancing in sweltering heat. The many bands included Methodist Boys' High School, Albert Academy Band and CMS Grammar School Band. There was the band of the Armed Forces of Sierra Leone which played at the reception in State House, hosted by the Governor-General Sir Henry Lightfoot-Boston and attended by the Prime Minister Sir Albert

Dr Pratt and Mr Albert Bayley (British Vice President),
view the autonomy scroll.

Margai and civic leaders both Muslim and Christian. The Mayor of Freetown, Mrs Constance Cummings-John, an ardent Methodist, brought greetings. The garden party at State House was the talk of the nation because Dr Pratt had requested that no alcohol be served. The dignitaries seemed to enjoy their soft drinks but the new Heineken Brewery at Kissy was not best pleased.

I was a probationer minister at the time, having arrived in the country in the previous year to study African religion and language at Fourah Bay College under the tutelage of Rev Professor Dr Canon Harry Sawyerr CBE. I attended the historic Conference, but strictly speaking, I was not a member. When the last Conference members had walked up the long aisle in Wesley Church to sign the illuminated scroll which came out of a long silver casket, I heard Dr Pratt call my name to sign the deed. It was a memorable indication of the generosity and grace for which the Methodist Church in Sierra Leone is well known.

The occasion went off very well with fullness of joy and at great length. A combined robed choir of 250 voices sang the praises of Jesus Christ. Rev Dr Frederick Greeves was able to preach after the inaugural service had continued for two hours. Visitors from other churches included Archbishop Moses N C O Scott (Anglican), Rev Dr S M Renner (EUB), Rev Clifford Gill (Baptist), Rev Fr. Liam Sullivan (Roman Catholic) and Rev Titus S Fewry (West African Methodist).

Young people took part in the Conference celebrations as well as senior ministers who had long since retired. Rev Eliab J T Harris, venerable looking with his bushy white hair and trumpet voice, called the Conference to prayer and to scriptural holiness.

The new Conference created two Districts, the Western District whose Chairman was Rev Prince A J Williams and the Provincial District whose chairman was Rev Sidney N Groves. The reigning political Party had as its motto: 'One Country, One People.' The church had a similar calling. Some Freetown ministers offered to be stationed in the Provincial District and a Mende minister was appointed to a Freetown Circuit. Creole leaders accepted membership on up-country Boards of Management at the hospital, schools and agricultural projects. Later two Creole ministers were elected to serve as Chairman of the Bo-Kenema District: Rev Ola E K Ferguson and Rev S Dowridge Williams. The new Methodist President and Vice-President travelled the country in spite of advancing years. There were still many missionaries and the welcome for them continued to be warm. Indeed local people were saddened when missionary families had to return to UK or Ireland for education of their children or to care for ageing parents.

The changes brought about by autonomy created more administrative work and gave lay members more responsibility. There was an increase in contacts with Government where there were Methodists among the Members of Parliament and Civil Service. Autonomy gave opportunities to collaborate with other Christian denominations to discuss matters of national concern and to make representation to the Head of State. Evangelism and church training expanded and the gospel reached into unevangelised areas of Guinea.

The Methodist Missionary Society was held in high regard. It had for many years caught the currents of the time and embraced a missionary policy propounded by Henry Venn which aimed for self-governing, self-supporting and self-propagating churches. The thrust of this policy was intended to encourage the africanisation of the church. The Methodist Missionary Society was actively supportive of Autonomy and handed over all its assets to the new Conference, retaining none. Although the Wesleyan Methodist Missionary Society (later known as Methodist Missionary Society, Methodist Church Overseas Division or World Church Office) had been involved in Sierra Leone since the early 1800s, it endeavoured to go about its work avoiding prevailing colonialist attitudes. Some colonialist regimes can be guilty of bearing their gifts proudly. The Missionary Society sought to follow the example of the wise men who brought their gifts to Jesus on bended knee.

The Autonomous Methodist Conference, under the leadership of Rev Dr Akinumi Pratt got off to a good start on its journey. He became the figurehead for the Methodist Church and was a courageous Christian voice to the nation as both these bodies moved forward in faith. In the Greek language, *Synod* has the meaning of journeying together on an odyssey. The Methodist Church, like every Christian was on a journey from the passing to the permanent and from the partial to the perfect. For this journey two things are needed - a guide who goes ahead and companions who travel alongside. Christ is our guide and believers are our company.

Using a different metaphor, Dr Pratt liked to describe Leslie as the architect of autonomy for the Methodist Church, Sierra Leone. The same phrase was used in an illuminated address presented to Leslie when he was leaving the country after 39 years of missionary service (see appendix B). It was a good time for faith and hope and love.

Laymen's Association 1970

Drafting a new Church Constitution

The newly drafted Constitution, Practice and Discipline (CPD) of the Methodist Church, Sierra Leone was passed unanimously at the start of the Inaugural Conference. The drafting team had done their work well.

The creation of the document was a herculean task and Leslie was the right person to take responsibility for the work. For this he studied other African Church Constitutions as well as documents from World Methodism including the Irish Methodist Conference. It was not his first entry into this legal territory for he had shared in the earlier drafting of a Constitution for the proposed Methodist Conference of West Africa. To this task he applied the meticulousness of a lawyer, the mind of a theologian and the wisdom of a Christian pastor. He knew it was a *magnum opus* but he never allowed his own contribution to be highlighted. It was God's work and others played their part. In the tradition of Methodist churches throughout the world, included in the Sierra Leone Methodist constitution were strictures forbidding the use of alcoholic wine during Holy Communion. The Methodist Church had long taken a stance against drinking alcohol.

At one point in this process, Leslie's briefcase was stolen in Freetown with some of these important documents and money. This was before the days of photocopiers and computers where you could have multiple copies and back-up records. Each draft was typed on a manual typewriter with carbon paper providing three or four copies or at best a stencil was cut for a Gestetner duplicator. An appeal was made on national radio and in the press for the return of the documents. God answered prayer and it was a cause of great thanksgiving when the documents were recovered, even without the money.

Another major task was the formation of Trustees of the Methodist Church. To this legal body was transferred all the properties and leases and finances that had been held in London by the Methodist Missionary Trust Account until the Conference was formed. Freetown solicitor Mr Hudson Harding and Justice Sir Emile Fashole Luke guided the church through this monumental task without payment. The properties to be transferred were numbered in hundreds. They included all churches, manses and leases. Also transferred were all school properties including Methodist Boys' High School and

Methodist Girls' High School, Bunumbu Teachers' College, Segbwema Hospital, the Provincial Literature Bureau at Bo, Methodist Church Headquarters at 11 Gloucester Street, the site at 4 George Street where the present Headquarters building is located and many more besides. The list of the Trustees was readily agreed by the inaugural Conference. A new Act of Parliament was gazetted which was called The Methodist Church Lands Act.

The transfer of monies and accounts from London to Freetown was expertly handled by Mr E R G Davies the first Conference Treasurer who set up many new accounts. He was aided by Mr Stanley Hall who lectured in Accountancy in Fourah Bay College. The officers of the Methodist Missionary Society in London were very helpful in this complex process. In the meantime there was another military *coup* in Freetown and it was the solicitor Mr Hudson Harding who advised that the Church should wait before registering the Trusts until the Military Government was out of power and a civilian Government was returned. It was the right advice. In the Conference office, the President was full time and the Secretary was part time. They were helped over the years by able administrators including Vera Adams, Elma Burness, Violet Martin, Mary Mawson and Mrs Frances Robin-Mason.

Rev Dr W E Akinumi Pratt OBE, first President of Conference

Rev Dr W E Akinumi Pratt, the first President of the newly Autonomous Church confessed that he was apprehensive about autonomy but accepted the idea that a dependent church in an independent country was an anomaly. The reasons for reluctance on the part of some in the Western Area with regard to autonomy may have been the severing of the sentimental historical links with Britain as 'the mother church' or concerns about financial support or an apprehension about the cohesion of the new Conference as it encompassed the disparate ethnic areas of Freetown and the Provinces. Dr Pratt stressed that the Methodist Church was accepting autonomy rather than independence because a church is always by nature dependent upon God's grace and was part of an inter-dependent world fellowship.

In the foreword to Dr Pratt's autobiography published in 1973 Leslie wrote the following:

"It is an honour to be invited to write a short foreword to the autobiography of Rev Dr W E A Pratt OBE, MA. For twenty-four years as his ministerial colleague I have been in close contact with Dr Pratt. It was a high privilege to be Secretary of Conference during his period of devoted service as the first President of the Methodist Church, Sierra Leone.

W.E. Akinumi Pratt was born in York village, Sierra Leone on 6th July 1897, the fifth of seven children of Jacob Rufus Pratt and Christiana Bernice Johnson. He enjoyed a full and happy boyhood. His account of early primary schooling in York and the competitive secondary school education in the United Methodist Collegiate School makes interesting and entertaining reading. He was a diligent student both at College and University from which he graduated Bachelor of Arts in 1921. He obtained the Diploma in Theology in 1922 and had his Master's degree conferred three years later. It was a great joy to his many friends when the University of Sierra Leone conferred on him the Doctorate of Divinity (honoris causa) in 1969.

In 1924 he began his service in the Methodist ministry and was ordained in 1929. He travelled in many circuits in the Western District and served for a short period at Tikonko where he opened a Training College which later developed into the Teacher Training College at Bunumbu. On 28th April 1932 he married Miss Josephine Agnes Remilekun Decker, a teacher, musician and gifted pianist. Being appointed Chairman and General Superintendent and later President of the first autonomous Conference was a surprise to him but not to his brethren and the Conference.

The names of Elkanah (which means 'whom God possessed') and Akinumi ('I admire the brave') have been lived up to in word and deed. Dr Pratt is a fearless and courageous preacher. For him evil does not change with time or person. He still proclaims the prophetic note: "thou art the man." In adversity he has been admired with the brave souls of our day and has borne his cross honourably."

During the time that Dr Pratt was President of the Conference there may have been as many as thirty missionary personnel working with the Methodist Church in evangelism, education, medicine and administration. Dr Pratt was a friend to all the missionaries. Verena Wallace always thought of him as her 'African grandfather.' The arrival of Dr Pratt on board the ships which brought the missionaries to Freetown was an unforgettable welcome and he would walk with the new arrivals down the gangplank and escort them through the customs.

In his autobiography Dr Pratt gives high praise to Leslie, the Irish man, for his "Trojan work." They were a perfect team together at a strategic time for the Church and the Nation. A vital part of the team was the first Vice-President Mr E J Robinson JP CH and after his two year appointment, he was followed by Lewis J Pratt, OBE, MA, MEd, who had served as a diplomat in London and was a man of learning, devotion, charm and wisdom. At a later date his distinguished wife Amy Pratt was elected to the Vice-Presidency, the first woman to hold the office.

It is true to say that some Creole members of Synod were hesitant about the africanisation of the church leadership. It is unclear why this was so. It may have been a fear that the support of the Mission House in London would lessen. Dr Pratt himself thought it was because some regarded him as 'a village boy' who was not from the original Creole ascendency. Notable Freetown personalities Rev E T Fyle and Dr I G Cummings spoke against the appointment of the first African Chairman of Synod. When a fractious Synod adjourned for lunch, Leslie offered to take Rev E T Fyle home for his lunch. Throughout the prolonged lunch break Mr Fyle and Leslie argued the *pros* and *cons* of indigenous leadership, the African arguing against it and the Irishman arguing for it. When Synod re-assembled after the siesta, there was general surprise when Rev E T Fyle supported the proposal for Dr Pratt to continue in office as Chairman and General Superintendent. It seems like "a word in season" had been spoken and heard.

Leading laypersons

The relationship between the ordained and unordained people of God is essential for the benefit of the work of God. The Krio proverb is apt: *Wan han noh de tai bondul* ("A bundle cannot be fastened with one hand"). If the church is to be the church it is vital that too sharp a distinction should not be made between ministers and laypersons. God gives gifts to his church, to ordained laity and unordained laity and the gifts of both are needed. Leslie was aware that occasionally in the Western Area, tensions arose in churches because of the extremes of clericalism and anti-clericalism. Christ's church is a community of people made distinctive by the call of God where privilege has been abolished and laity do not lord it over ministers nor do ministers lord it over laity. The church is called to unity in diversity like St. Paul's analogy of a single human body made up of many parts: "As in one body we have many members, and all the members do not have the same function, so we, though many, are one body in Christ, and individually members one of another. Having gifts that differ according to the grace given to us, let us use them" (Romans 12: 4-6). Charles Wesley expressed this in a hymn: "The gift which he on one bestows, we all delight to prove."

It was Methodist practice to include lay persons in ministry and in church governance, alongside ordained ministers in a collaborate leadership. The Methodist Church believes in the priesthood of all believers. In the New Testament the term 'Priest' belongs to Christ (Hebrews 9:11) and to Christians in general (1 Peter 2:9). It is nowhere given to describe a leader in Christian service. Accordingly, Leslie encouraged opening the communion rail to include lay Conference officials or local preachers inside it. This seems a simple matter and it was common practice in the Provincial District and in the City Mission but was not generally common in the Western Area. Leslie persisted in an open communion rail although opposed by such worthies as Rev S Dowridge Williams, a future President. Likewise in the matter of admission to the Lord's Supper he distanced himself from a tendency among some ministers to use admission to the Lord's Table as a matter of discipline and preferred to see admission to the sacrament as a means of grace.

Sometimes in Freetown churches, dress for worship could be a sensitive matter. Leslie dressed decently and neatly. He began using local tailors to make his suits and to sew clerical attire of local material. If queried about his departure from traditional wearing of Victorian or Edwardian suits at Sunday worship in Freetown, he could quote the scripture 1 Samuel 16:7 "But the Lord said to Samuel, 'Do not consider his appearance or his height, for I have rejected him. The Lord does not look at the things man looks at. Man looks at the outward appearance, but the Lord looks at the heart.' This liberalisation was welcomed by

Provincial Synod 1967

the younger generation and in Freetown, Rev Dr Leslie Shyllon led the way, with others, in the use of African dress by ministers in the pulpit.

Leslie constantly admired the work of gifted Sunday school teachers, women's workers, class leaders, local preachers, school teachers, stewards, trustees, treasurers and many more officials. He has a list of several pages noting the names of those with whom he worked. They are too many to be mentioned. An exception will be made for those who shared in the historic events surrounding the inaugural Conference.

Mr E.L. Coker OBE had abilities to grace any international corporation yet he was content to freely serve as a Church Steward in Freetown and as honorary Conference Treasurer. He was a member of the World Methodist Council who insisted on paying his own way. His son is a doctor in Freetown and his daughter is a faithful member of the Conference finance committee and her signature appears on Sierra Leone banknotes.

Mrs Fashu Collier was the Principal of Methodist Girls' High School in Freetown and the school prospered in every way under her leadership. She was a cultured lady and her impressive reports to the annual Synod or Conference were presented with professionalism. There was healthy rivalry between The Methodist Girls' High School (founded 1880) and the Methodist Boys' High School (founded 1874 with eight pupils. Creole minister, Rev Joseph Claudius May, was its first Principal).

Mrs Frances Robin-Mason worked at the Conference Headquarters as an able administrator and trained new members of staff as the work of the Conference increased.

Mr G L Thomas was Controller of Income Tax for the Government and served as secretary of the Conference Finance committee, where he worked hard each year on preparing the finance documents for Conference. He was a local preacher with a sharp intellect and a humble spirit and was a respected colleague.

Mr S A Palmer was the Government Printer and a Circuit Steward in Wilberforce. He was a helpful man to have on committees and was President of the Local Preachers' Mutual Aid Association. He printed the annual Almanac which contained readings for each Sunday service as well as photographs of Connexional events all over the country. Churches and homes all over the land, fine houses and humble huts, would have the Methodist Almanac hang on the wall.

Dr Taylor Cummings was an active member of the Methodist Hospital Management Committee where his wisdom guided the hospital in challenging times.

Dr Sama Banya from Kailahun, studied medicine in England and opened medical practice in Kenema. He was an effective local preacher and later served as Foreign Minister and Vice-President of the country. His friend and fellow Conference member was Mr Braima S Massaquoi, a Christian convert who would later serve as a Government minister. At a time when competition between the two rival parties was bitter, and sometimes violent, both of these men at the annual Methodist Conference and in the Kenema Methodist Church made a point of sitting together and they would kneel together at the Lord's Table and partake in the Lord's Supper. In Kenema, Rev Richard Jackson was pastor to these leaders, and with his wife Carole, a medical doctor, was a friend. Richard Jackson recalls events in 1977 when both Dr Sama S Banya, a local preacher and Mr B S Massaquoi, a church leader had put themselves forward as candidates for Parliament, one for the All Peoples Congress Party and the other for the Sierra Leone Peoples Party. Violence broke out during the electioneering. People were killed and Forest Industries, a major employer in Kenema, was burnt to the ground.

On the Sunday after Easter as the recriminations began and revenge was being sought, the two Methodist friends from opposing Parties, Dr Banya and Mr Massaquoi stood side by side in Kenema Methodist church appealing for peace. By the time the elections took place on the 6th May 1977, B S Massaquoi had been beaten up and Dr Banya had been caught in an ambush in which his brother was killed and he himself was shot and had head wounds. Rumour had spread that Dr Banya had been killed and this caused further unrest. Leslie personally notified the Vice President of the country that Dr Banya was alive in the Methodist Mission Hospital at Segbwema. Mr S I Koroma sent his Cuban helicopter pilots to bring Dr Banya to Freetown and his life was saved.

The good news at the end of that particular story was that both Dr Banya and B S Massaquoi were elected to parliament and went on to serve faithfully for a number of years. Tragically, during the rebel war 1991-2002, Mr B S Massaquoi was mercilessly beaten and killed on 8th February 1998 in Kenema and his body was buried in a mass grave. Thousands of other brave and innocent people suffered horrible fates in an era that is painful to remember. Sierra Leoneans do, however, possess an amazing capacity for forgiveness and can put personal tragedy in the perspective of society at large.

Besides those Lay Vice-Presidents of Conference already mentioned, others were involved at the time of autonomy. W N Mends was a leader in Freetown Methodism. G Y Macauley was a teacher and education secretary who became Vice-President and was later ordained and made Chairman of the Bo-Kenema District. John S Koker was the son of a Paramount Chief who forbade his children to be baptised. The children, however, including John, faithfully followed Christ and later on John was an effective Vice-President of Conference.

Many teachers heard God's call to ordained ministry and included Rev Christian V A Peacock, who later became President of the Conference having been the first non-stipendiary minister. While Freetown was well-served by a long succession of Creole ministers during 150 years of Christian witness, the first Limba minister and the first three Mende ministers were received in the 1950s. They were D M Karanke, P F Jibao, S M Musa and D D Tucker. These came from the ranks of teachers.

Sometimes our teachers, both indigenous and expatriate, were not given enough recognition in the expansion of the Christian Mission. F. F. Bruce says in his commentary on Hebrews: "Christianity is sacrificial through and through; it is founded on the one self-offering of Christ. The offering of His people's praise and property, of their service and their lives, is caught up into the perfection of His acceptable sacrifice, and is accepted in Him." Without the Christian, sacrificial, willing service of these laypersons whose names have been mentioned and the thousands of others whom they represent, the church would not be the church.

A new Headquarters building

For many years the Methodist Church Headquarters building was at 11 Gloucester Street, Freetown, which was a distinctive Creole building with stone foundations, wooden superstructure with shutters, balcony and tin roof. It had three floors providing modest office and guest facilities and was central to the General Post Office across the street. The Methodist Church also owns the McFoy estate adjacent to the CMS bookshop and planned to develop the site. Instead a decision was taken to build on the site in George Street beside the Anglican Cathedral. This Conference Headquarters building would include extra floors which could be leased to businesses and from the rents received, the expenses of the Conference administration would be paid without being an assessment on the Church Circuits. The arrangement was that one third of rental income was set aside for the upkeep of the building while two thirds would pay for the Conference administration.

The building was well constructed by the Lebanese firm of Casas. The architect and the surveyor were Mr George Lewis and Mr Alex Browne respectively, both well known in Freetown Methodism and they served our church generously and expertly in this project. The Missionary Society in London gave a financial grant which paid for the construction of the building. This substantial amount was gratefully received and would reduce the annual grant from London. Leslie took delight in responding to anyone who asked him: "Where is the Anglican Cathedral in Freetown?" and his answer would be: "It is beside the Methodist Church Headquarters!" The first tenants were the German Embassy whose annual payment of £10,000 sterling was paid by agreement to the Sierra Leone Methodist Accounts at the Midland Bank, London. Being paid in sterling it did not suffer currency fluctuations.

CHAPTER 8

FREETOWN CITY MISSION

Having been appointed as Secretary for the newly autonomous Conference of the Methodist Church, Leslie was moved from Bo and was stationed at the Freetown City Mission in September 1968 in the Balmer Memorial Church which was multi-lingual in English, Mende and Krio. He replaced Rev Francis Marratt. City Missions of the Methodist Church, sometimes called 'Central Missions,' are visible expressions of social and community concern by local congregations. They are to be found in large cities throughout the world. Sometimes they incorporate a large auditorium which is called 'Central Hall.'

The Mende City Mission building had been constructed with generous financial help from the Methodist philanthropist, Lady Kelly, from Bangor, Northern Ireland. The building was named after Rev W T Balmer, a missionary and a distinguished theologian who was the first Principal of Richmond College in Sierra Leone 1901-1909. He had also served as College Principal in the Gold Coast before returning to

Sierra Leone in 1914 where colleges were amalgamated and he became Vice-Principal of Fourah Bay College as well as Principal of The High School. He encouraged evangelisation of the Mendeland at a time when Freetown churches were not so missionary-minded.

The capital city would open up a whole new set of opportunities and challenges for Christian service in the Kingdom of God. The Wallace family resided at Two Trees Compound on the Old Railway Line adjacent to Methodist Girls' High School. Agnes played the organ at Hill Station church. Verena attended the International School before going as a boarder to Methodist College Belfast.

The City Mission was involved in distributing social aid to those who had arrived in Freetown from up-country finding themselves without jobs and sometimes food and shelter. They were the hapless poor who fall beneath the city's reach. When Leslie was queried by a colleague about giving money to people begging on the streets, he offered the reply: "You never know, you may be helping Jesus." This was in the tradition of Rev John Wesley who, in his sermon 'On pleasing all men' said: "A poor wretch cries to me for an alm: I look, and see him covered with dirt and rags. But through these I see one that has an immortal spirit made to know, and love, and dwell with God in eternity. I honour him for his Creator's sake." The Mission tackled poverty and the causes of poverty. The holistic gospel emphasised the redemption of souls and the need to redeem cultures lest they become depraved without the light and love of God. When Jesus said: "Go into all the world" (Matthew 28:19) it was an instruction to evangelise every area of life in every place. Freetown City Mission maintained this balanced approach in its mission between the personal gospel and the social gospel. The life and mission of Jesus Christ is like his robe, seamless and woven from the top throughout.

Almost unnoticed, the name 'Mende City Mission' became 'Freetown City Mission' as it sought to reach out to any who needed Christ and charity. Senesie Fallah and his wife Agnes Bonya who was the women's worker at the City Mission assisted in the social work. As well as feeding the hungry, Agnes Bonya collected bottles and filled them with home-made ginger cordial in an effort to provide an alternative to alcohol which was causing havoc in many homes in Freetown. She was the first Mende woman to be appointed to represent Sierra Leone at the British

Methodist Conference. When asked to share in opening devotions in that formidable gathering she spontaneously led the extempore singing of the Sankey hymn: "I am so glad that our Father in heaven tells of his love in the book he has given. Wonderful things in the Bible I see, this is the dearest that Jesus loves me."

Another colleague was sent to the City Mission when Conference responsibilities became heavy. Rev Abayomi B Cole was an enthusiastic witness for his Saviour and was a cheerful, Godly man whose constant references to "Papa God" earned him the nickname 'Papa God' Cole. The two ministers worked well together with great mutual respect. Many were saved, prodigals returned to God and families were helped.

It was said by Arnold Lunn that: "John Wesley was so obsessed by the eternal values that he completely lost all sense of class values." The same could be said of Leslie. His calling was to offer Christ to the down and outs and to the up and outs as he went about his ministry sharing God's indiscriminate love.

A busy life required a disciplined life-style. Leslie was diligent in the spiritual exercises which Methodist piety emphasised including private prayer, Bible study, worship, fellowship, fasting, works of mercy and evangelism.

As Secretary of Conference he approached all his tasks with graciousness, consistency, patience and forward planning. His quiet dynamism, his accurate memory, his attention to detail and an ability to work with people stood him in good stead in this work. Administration is a charismatic gift from God and is listed among the gifts of the Holy Spirit in 1 Corinthians 12:28. The word 'administration' appears only once in the New Testament, and carries the meaning of a helmsman who steers a ship to its destination. The Conference recognised in him the ability to keep the church on course toward the accomplishment of God's mission. Such leadership required the qualities of vision, industry, perseverance, service and discipline. His leadership was non-directive in style.

In committees at the City Mission or at Conference, where he was often either secretary or chair, everyone was allowed their say while he patiently held his counsel. When all members had spoken, Leslie would quietly offer to summarise the discussion and steer the meeting towards a proposal which more often than not became the minuted decision. His effectiveness as a leader was enhanced by the fact that he was blessed with ample common sense, a great gift from God. Occasionally he might have concluded a discussion with a magisterial pronouncement but it was always seasoned with grace.

CHAPTER 9

UNITED CHRISTIAN COUNCIL OF SIERRA LEONE

Leslie knew that there was only one church, the world church. He was elected Chairman of the United Christian Council of Sierra Leone which is now called the Council of Churches, Sierra Leone (CCSL). The council was formed in response to a perceived need for a united prophetic voice for the Christian churches and missions to be presented to Government. It remained above Party politics. Ecumenical relations between the churches were cordial if cool and cooperation was a matter of spiritual unity rather than organic union. As well as the United Christian Council there was the Sierra Leone Evangelical Fellowship. There were a few interdenominational congregations. Hill Station Church was interdenominational and so was the united evangelical service held in Zion Wilberforce Street each Sunday evening. In social and educational matters the collaboration was more vigorous.

The UCC was a good vehicle for channelling relief aid to refugees such as those fleeing unrest in Liberia at the time of the assassination of President Tolbert in 1980 and more recently during the time of the rebel war 1991-2002. In 1980 mercy ships from Ghana and Nigeria unloaded supplies in Freetown harbour and the UCC shared responsibility for their transport and distribution. Again, all of this was done in the name of God who "upholds the cause of the oppressed and gives food to the hungry" (Psalm 146:7).

It was also an umbrella organisation for the Education Departments of the member churches. Government would not authorise schools of any church that was not a member of UCC. This widened the representation of the UCC to include the Pentecostal, Independent and New Churches. The Roman Catholic Church was unable to join the UCC because it was not united with the other churches. However the Catholics were co-operative in social matters and generously contributed relief materials and transport. In general, in those times after the second Vatican Council, relations between Roman Catholics and Protestants were active and amicable although low key. Leslie was pleased to accept invitations, on several occasions, to lead Bible studies at the annual retreat for the Holy Ghost Fathers. In the area of medical work and the training of nurses and midwives there was full co-operation. There was close co-operation in Army chaplaincy and in prison ministries. In the area of education there was undoubted competition between the two communions. The rapid rise of Methodist Secondary Schools in the Provinces may well have been a reaction to Roman Catholic expansion into areas where there was no RC primary school yet Catholic secondary schools were being built.

Interfaith relations were also a concern of the United Christian Council. Leslie recalls an occasion at State house when he was representing the United Christian Council at the swearing in ceremony of new Government ministers. The Chief Imam was also there representing the Muslims. Before the ceremony, the Vice President of Sierra Leone called for drinks to be served. The Imam whispered to Leslie that he did not consume alcohol. Leslie, also a strict teetotaller, explained that they would like a drink of orange. There was none available and the proceedings were held up for some time until the two glasses of orange arrived ceremoniously and the proceedings could begin.

Relations between Muslims and Christians were mild rather than aggressive. There was one notable exception to this respectful accommodation. On one occasion at Easter in Freetown, a Muslim group of the Ahmadiyya tradition, burned a Bible, made mockery of a cross and produced some anti-Christian leaflets. This sent shockwaves throughout the Christian community and caused some concern to Government. The United Christian Council arranged to meet the leaders of the Muslim Communities in Freetown in the building which housed the offending printing press. A *modus vivendi* was eventually agreed and no such inter-faith aggression re-occurred. An amusing thing happened as the church leaders left the building. One

1st meeting of West Africa Methodist Council c.1954

of the printing staff recognised Leslie and knew of his expertise with Heidelberg printing machines. He asked for his help with a broken-down printing machine. A simple half turn of a screw was all that was needed and Leslie searched in his pocket for a nail file but he felt that the Lord told him to leave the nail file in his pocket!

Leslie saw the United Christian Council as a tool for spreading the Kingdom of God. He was able to further the work of two organisations close to his heart. The first of these was the United Bible Society doing translation and literacy work. Likewise the Provincial Literature Bureau in Bo, though Methodist in origin, came under the umbrella of the UCC and promoted literature in the vernacular employing colporteurs selling Bibles and books in the vernacular. The Church Missionary Society Bookshop in Freetown was a partner in promoting the sale of Bibles and literature in local languages with supportive managers like Fred Ward and Ted Stapleford. The Scripture Union and Christian Literature Crusade Bookshop promoted scripture sales.

The other organisation which Leslie encouraged through the UCC was the Boys' Brigade Movement with Mr Sesay as its National organiser and Mr Norman as its leader in Freetown. This was a time of expansion for the Boys' Brigade throughout the country and not least in Methodist Schools. The object of the Boys' Brigade is: "The advancement of Christ's Kingdom among boys and the promotion of habits of obedience, reverence, discipline and self-respect and all that tends towards true Christian manliness." BB was a uniformed marching organisation which seemed to prosper in former British Colonies.

The United Christian Council was active in the world outside the church because its leaders believed that the world belonged to God. It is not the devil's world. The devil may have hijacked the world but he does not own it. Members of the UCC were inspired by examples of courageous church leaders who stood up for Godly principles in their own countries. Such leaders were Germany's Dietrich Bonhoeffer, El Salvador's Archbishop Oscar Romero, Uganda's Archbishop Janani Jakaliya Luwum, Rhodesia's Andrew Ndhlela and South Africa's Archbishop Desmond Tutu. These were examples of Christian ministers bringing God's transforming love into oppressive political situations. The Christ they knew and followed was the Saviour for all of life, for all time and for all of the world.

The Council of Methodist Churches of West Africa

By 1954 the British Methodist Church had five District Synods in West Africa: The Gambia, Sierra Leone, The Gold Coast, Western Nigeria and Eastern Nigeria. In addition there was the work in the French territories of Ivory Coast, Dahomey and Togoland. At that time there was serious consideration being given to the formation of an international autonomous Conference called "The Methodist Church in West Africa." The Sierra Leone representatives on the planning committee were Rev H T Cooke, Rev S L Wallace (Assistant Secretary of the committee) and Mr W N Mends. A detailed Constitution was drawn up and discussed during the next few years. A vote was taken to form a Methodist Church of West Africa and all the national representatives agreed except the two largest synods, The Gold Coast and Nigeria. They preferred to travel towards national church autonomy and without them the project was impracticable. However the work was not wasted. The work on the constitution became a document of reference for Conferences which were preparing for autonomy in nations with territorial independence.

The West Africa Methodist Council continued as a useful forum for Methodist Churches in the region. The Council shared resources for local preacher training, mission strategies, ecumenical relations and ministerial training. Its first meeting was in Freetown and Rev Dr Grant of Ghana was its chairman, Rev T Wallace Koomson (Ghana) was secretary and Leslie was his assistant. It was a time when the Methodist Church expanded rapidly in West African nations. Theological Colleges co-operated across national borders, facilitated by Rev Hugh Thomas from Trinity College, Legon in Accra and theological papers were printed and distributed throughout West Africa. Local preaching was standardised across the region. I was appointed an examiner for West Africa and I remember receiving in the post hundreds of manuscripts, twice a year from local preachers on trial. These numbers were somewhat swelled by fifth and sixth form students of religion, in Ghana and Nigeria who sat the Methodist local preachers exams as a matter of course.

The Council ceased to exist when Methodist Churches attained autonomy and when the cost of travel became a burden.

The World Methodist Council

The Methodist Church had work in 132 countries. It included in its executive, Sierra Leonean leaders, both ordained and lay. John Wesley once said that the Methodist people were one people. Sierra Leone had recorded the first Methodists in Africa among the freed slaves in 1792 with 223 members. In 2011 there are an estimated 30 million Methodists in Africa out of a total of 79 million throughout the world. Leslie with others represented Sierra Leone Methodism on this body. The WMC existed to promote effective use of Methodist resources in the Christian mission, encourage evangelism, promote Christian education, pray for and support needs of persecuted Christians and encourage ministries of justice and peace. It strongly opposed the Apartheid policies of the South African government.

All-Africa Council of Churches

As Christianity expanded throughout the continent, the All-Africa Council of Churches became a voice for African Christians. Leslie recalls attending an AACC literacy workshop held in Kitwe in Zambia in 1970. He travelled with three African colleagues from Ghana, Nigeria and Dahomey. They had trouble with the Apartheid Government when travelling through South Africa to Zambia so they decided to go home by another route, this time through Congo. However, when they arrived in Congo they were stranded in the airport at Elizabethville for 24 hours and were hungry. Leslie was standing outside the airport when a platoon of United Nations Peace-Keeping soldiers marched past. He noticed from the shamrocks on their shoulder patches that they were Irish peace-keeping troops so he began to whistle the tune: "In Dublin's fair city, where the girls are so pretty." Later the platoon Sergeant came back to the airport and greeted him with the words: "What are you doing here, Paddy?" The sergeant then arranged to send Leslie and his colleagues a basin of very sweet hot chocolate and some mugs. Eventually he arrived back in Freetown via Jos and Lagos and Accra. Literacy and Bible Translation were still Leslie's passion and were worth any delays or such inconveniences.

Rev Arnold C Temple, a future President of the Methodist Church, Sierra Leone, served as Executive Secretary of the All Africa Council of Churches having worked in Kitwe and Nairobi.

CHAPTER 10

FREETOWN – CHAPLAINCIES

At a time when there were hundreds of international volunteer workers in the country serving with such organisations such as Voluntary Service Overseas (VSO) or Peace Corps, Agnes and Leslie seemed to be providing an unofficial *ad hoc* international chaplaincy. Expatriates who needed advice, hospitality or rescue, received assistance. Many benefited from contacts with Government Departments, the Passport Office and travel bureaux and will always be grateful.

Prisons ministry

In an official capacity Leslie was appointed visiting Chaplain to prisons on 1 Nov 1968. For almost 20 years he quietly ministered to the prisoners of Pademba Road Gaol, among those condemned to seclusion and deprivation.

Rev Jesa Williams, retired Chaplain-General in the forces, Correctional Chaplain Sierra Leone Prisons and Chief Advisor to Army Chaplains, writes of his early training by both Rev Leslie Wallace and Rev Mano Williams.

"When I received my letter of appointment as the prison and correctional service's chaplain, I went to the army chaplains, to Rev Major Mano Davis and the Rev S L Wallace, who was a civilian chaplain, a Methodist minister and member of the Council of Churches Sierra Leone and it was here with these men that my chaplaincy work really started to take shape....Sunday in the prisons were always very hectic....The Rev Wallace had by then, taught me how to approach prisoners in their cells, to make visits to the newly sentenced prisoners, as well as long-term and also the condemned prisoners and also how to assist those who were sick in the hospital. Even though I was an officer who had been trained at college, the experiences of these two men was far beyond what I could offer but they shared it with me and showed me the way for over 50 years of service in chaplaincy."

Leslie helped condemned prisoners make their peace with God and stayed with them until their execution. He sought clemency for those on death row and on occasion this caused tension between himself and the Head of State, especially when the condemned men were senior army officers allegedly involved in a political *coup d'état*.

In 1967, at the time of political turmoil, the country was governed by the National Reformation Council which came to power by a military *coup d'état*. Some younger army officers in training were recalled from Sandhurst and Mons. Brigadier Juxon-Smith, the Head of the military *junta*, and others were later ousted and accused of treason and condemned to death. The situation was tense in the country. When Leslie visited them in prison it was his custom always to read from the book of Psalms, a scripture which the Muslims present acknowledged. He would also read from the gospels. The Muslim officers would stand to attention while their Christian colleagues shared in the Holy Communion. Religious leaders signed a petition for clemency to the Head of State. Leslie drafted the document and hastily collected signatures of Church leaders and Muslim representatives. He recalls Archbishop Moses Scott signing the document in the street using the bonnet of the car as a desktop. The Petition requesting clemency was successful on this occasion. On another occasion a similar plea went unheeded when Brigadier-General John Bangura who forcibly took over as Governor General of Sierra Leone for a few months in 1968 was later executed in Pademba Road prison, together with some other army officers in March 1970. Leslie was asked by the condemned men to pray with them and to give them Holy Communion before they were led to the scaffold. The chaplains were not allowed to be present at the gallows. This denial of pastoral ministry was a matter of dispute between Leslie and the Head of State, Dr Siaka Stevens. Years later when Dr Siaka Stevens was retiring as Head of State he spoke of two

Going to the West Africa Methodist Council meeting in Lagos c.1956.
L-R: Rev S L Wallace; Mr Bismark Johnston (Mayor of Freetown); Rev W T Harris; Rev Jeremiah J Pratt

regrets. He regretted the closing of the railway and "certain executions."

Some school boys were arrested after a *fracas* at an inter-schools athletics championship in the national stadium. They were visited in prison by Leslie and were later released. Many years after this event, Leslie was in London and attended worship in Hinde Street Methodist Church and the steward at the door, distributing hymnbooks was one of these boys. Leslie cannot remember the sermon but he remembers the joyful welcome at the door!

On another occasion, Leslie's friend Dr Sama Banya, who later became Vice-President of Sierra Leone, was incarcerated, with others, in Pademba Road at a time of political tension. It was Christmas and Leslie was busy with church services in Freetown. Dr Banya who was a local preacher, not knowing that Leslie was on his way, conducted Christmas worship for the prisoners in his block.

Two churches in Ireland sent boxes of re-conditioned Methodist hymn books for use in the prisons. Inside the flyleaf of each hymnal

Award of M.B.E. by the British High Commissioner together with other members of the order.

was a rubber-stamped inscription: "Holywood Methodist Church" or "Newtownards Methodist Church." When two prisoners were being discharged and their particulars were being recorded, they were asked about their religious affiliation and they both affirmed that they belonged to "Holywood Methodist Church!"

Leslie had a portable Communion set contained in a small green case which he always brought with him into prison. He secured medicines for prisoners, not least at a time when some were dying of beri-beri. At other times letters and reading material for the inmates were made available. The prison authorities welcomed pastoral visits. They encouraged the participation by inmates in the learning of skills such as woodwork, agriculture and literacy. There was an occasion when Amnesty International wrote a damning report about the prisons in Sierra Leone. It caused a stir. While many of its criticisms were valid, Leslie thought that it ignored the positive work of some prison staff. Father Hennahan from the Holy Ghost Missionaries was one who worked to great effect to meet the huge humanitarian need in the prisons.

Army chaplaincy

On 19 Jan 1968 Leslie was appointed Officiating Chaplain to the Republic of Sierra Leone Military Forces (Other Denominations) Freetown Area. It was another means of sharing the gospel and showing God's love to a new set of people. He served in this role for almost 20 years, preaching at parade grounds and pastoring individuals and families at home and in hospital. Senior officers as well as rank and file soldiers knew him as a friend. Government ministers listened to him. At times of crisis involving the army, he sought to act behind the scenes as peacemaker in the name of Christ. Wherever he went throughout the country, he could pass through military road blocks unmolested.

On the occasion of an annual Sierra Leone Armed Forces day there was a church parade to College Chapel Methodist Church. Leslie was the preacher. A well-meaning church steward saw that the Secretary of the Ex-servicemen's Association was appointed to read the lesson and protested to Leslie that this was inappropriate because the man was a Muslim. Leslie explained that the steward should be glad that a Muslim was reading the Bible. The steward sat outside the church in protest and would not go in. The lesson was read well. Before the reader began, after the manner of Islam, he took off his shoes, cleansed his lips, removed his hat and read the Christian scriptures with respect and clarity.

When President Joseph Momoh, a former Major-General in the army, became Head of State he remembered Leslie's good work as Officiating Chaplain to the armed forces. They spoke together about re-instating army chaplaincy and arranged for the training of new chaplains, paid for by Government but accountable to their own churches.

CHAPTER 11

PRESIDENT OF THE CONFERENCE

Leslie was elected as President of the Methodist Church Sierra Leone, on three occasions and acted in the same capacity for one year making a total of twelve years in all. It may be that he would have preferred to remain as Secretary of Conference and serve in the background but such was the humility of the man that he graciously accepted the honour and responsibility that was thrust upon him since that was the will of the Methodist Conference by an overwhelming vote. Sometimes positions of public office are sought for personal aggrandisement and power. The Christian uses positions of responsibility as opportunities for the Master's service. The Conference obviously thought that Leslie was acceptable to both Districts and would be best able to continue the bridge-building work begun by Dr Pratt.

Rev Dr Pratt wrote about the election of his successor:

> "Some people have questioned me saying: 'Why did you choose a white man as your successor and not a black man' or to put it better, a European and not an African? My answer has always been that our Constitution knows no colour or tribe. It says: 'any minister of the Conference who is ten years and over after nomination can be nominated and appointed as President of the Conference.' To effect this, as I have said earlier, a blank voting paper is given annually to every member of Conference who is asked to put the best person to be the President of Conference. This was done and the European had an overwhelming majority. It is the Lord's doing and it is marvellous in our eyes. There was not the slightest possibility of rigging the nomination or appointment, no extra voting papers to carry in one's bosom, no campaigning speech or whisper. Without being misunderstood, I think the appointment of the European, the Rev S Leslie Wallace, is a big 'thank you' for the yeoman's work he did in connection with our autonomy. If anything, it is a feather in the cap of the thinking capability of the Sierra Leone Methodist Church."

Rev Dr W E Akinumi Pratt served three years as President of Conference and retired. When Leslie became President of Conference he gave his opening address from the text 1 Peter 4:17: "The time has come for the judgement to begin, it is beginning with God's own household." He stated that:

> "The church must always live its life, open to the judgement of God and it must be willing to be reformed in accordance with God's will. The reformation of the church is a continuing process and not just confined to the 16th century in Europe. God's living Spirit deals with us today as we face fresh opportunities to serve the present age. The people of God must be purged continually and remade. We must expect constant renewal and our attitude must include constant repentance. We are called to look inwards so that we may be more effective in the proclamation of the truth that God loves us not because we are good but because He is love.

Some conference members 1970

We are called to look to God for our help is in the Lord God. This leads us to examine our forms of worship; to re-structure our fellowship meetings and organisations in some of which there is too little Bible instruction or prayer. We are called to be open to the Holy Spirit who will lead us out from our buildings to meet the people in their farms, homes, villages and towns throughout the country, sharing the gospel with those who do not know the Saviour and caring for all with the compassion of Christ. We will be sensitive to the Holy Spirit who leads us to work with other Christians in joint action, renewed mission and unity of purpose. We place ourselves and our work under the judgement of the Tri-une God, for renewal. May the Church be so endowed with the heavenly wisdom that it may strengthen all who come into its fellowship and, by its teaching, guide them in the way of Christ."

Early Vice-Presidents, after E J Robinson and L J Pratt, were W N Mends and Mrs Amy Pratt, all of whom served for the two year period. Leslie served for the ensuing five years and then handed over to Rev Prince A.J. Williams. Sadly on 1st April 1975, the day of the hand-over, Mr Williams took ill. Arrangements were made for him to have medical treatment in the UK. His illness was terminal and he died on his return to Freetown. The funeral of 'PAJ' was one of the largest ever seen in the country. At his request he was buried in a plain coffin made by the prisoners of Pademba Road gaol.

Leslie continued in office for a further year at the end of which Conference elected him for another five years. He was then succeeded by Rev Nelson H Charles, a Sierra Leonean who had been received by the British Conference in London and who had transferred to the Sierra Leone Conference. Leslie was reappointed Secretary of Conference. There was a further crisis in stationing ministers at the end of the five-year Presidency of Rev Nelson Charles and Leslie was elected President for one final year being succeeded by Rev Gershon F H Anderson. It is worth noting the ease with which the Methodist Conference could vote and hand over the baton of office every five years or so. The Methodists seem to avoid the distress of some relay teams who lose out by dropping the baton at the hand-over. The voting, by ballot, was done without nominations or speeches. The Methodist Church had spoken out against the Head of State claiming election for life. It therefore would not contemplate that the election of the Methodist President should be for life. It was a Roman Catholic layman, Lord Acton, when speaking against the decree of papal infallibility in 1870 who said: "All power tends to corrupt and absolute power corrupts absolutely."

These years saw the Methodist Church grow rapidly especially in the Provinces. There was the danger of spreading so fast that there was little depth. It is possible for the church to be growing in numbers while deteriorating spiritually. A church leader in Tanzania has spoken of the challenges facing rapidly growing churches which were: the prosperity gospel, dream-based faith, poor leadership and lack of consistency. The words of Isaiah 54:2 are apt: "Lengthen your cords and strengthen your stakes.

Schools and churches were being opened at a great rate and ordinations were taking place for candidates for the itinerant ministry and for the local non-stipendiary ministry, both women and men. With the triumphant times there were struggles. Leslie was astute, strict and fair. On one occasion he was travelling to a village preaching appointment along the Freetown peninsula with the Superintendent of the Kent Circuit. When they came to the village of Sussex it became apparent that the Circuit Superintendent had never been to the village because he took him to the Anglican Church by mistake. Leslie was not amused.

There was pleasing unity within the Conference and yet there were occasions for discipline to be administered at minor synods. Holiness has been described as: "doing the right thing, in the right way, with the right spirit for the right motive." The spirit of holiness is perfect love. On this highway to holiness there are highs and lows and the church was journeying to maturity *via* mountain tops and through valleys.

John Goatley recalls the occasion of the attempted *coup* of 1971 in Freetown. During the Conference morning session, bullets were flying in Wesley Street outside Zion Church which was not far from Parliament Buildings. The Ministerial Session was closed quickly amid the sound of gunfire. The British visitor to Conference that year was Rev Vincent Parkin, Principal of Edgehill College, Belfast. He advised that the stations and the stipends be swiftly approved and that the General Purposes committee be authorised to complete the business at a later date. John Goatley remembers that: "Leslie closed down Conference with the utmost calm and reassurance, setting the tone for reassembling the General Purposes Committee later, when the military coup had failed and Prime Minister Siaka Stevens was back in power." Mr Parkin had been a Royal Air Force chaplain and could identify the type of rifle fire in the street outside. No one else was impressed. We all have our memories of leaving the church, amid the gunfire. Leslie remembers exiting the church and going to the crossroads to act as a traffic policeman as schoolchildren were fleeing and traffic was grid-locked. After lunch, Leslie told John Goatley that he would have to return downtown in case any lay Conference members had turned up for the afternoon session. John accompanied him back to Zion Church. "As we drove down, the streets were totally deserted and all shops were closed and shuttered. We met one army truck filled with soldiers, and as we held up our clerical collars they all cheered!" The leaders of this failed coup were convicted and executed, including several army officers and some senior government officials. Leslie quietly visited them in prison and at their request prayed with them before their deaths.

Within the Conference the two Districts were integrating. Change

Some ministers at Conference 1972 with the British Conference representative Rev Dr Kenneth Crosby

and convergence happened slowly because churches tend to be conservative. The Methodist Presidents, like Dr Pratt, needed to be good bridge-builders. The language, lifestyles and worship practices were different in the Provincial District and the Western District. Freetown churches were formerly draped in black for funerals and the reading desk was turned sideways instead of facing the congregation. Liturgical renewal was now taking place in all the churches. Younger ministers and young lay people began to assume leadership. They were not afraid to explore fresh expressions of church. They dressed for church in African style rather than European. Influenced by the writings of John Mbiti, Bolaji Idowu and Andrew Walls they were confidently stepping out of a Western Church culture into their African culture. Drums were appearing in worship services where formerly they were regarded as devilish. Translation needs to be both linguistic and cultural. The gospel message is unchanging but the way we 'do' church changes. Since the Acts of the Apostles the church had embraced cultural diversity. New African songs and 'shouts' accompanied by dance were enlivening worship in Freetown. It was a time to believe the Bible, care for the church and to champion change. The challenge was to find the proper balance between the old and the new, the ancient and the modern, the organ and the drums. This was an opportunity rather than a problem. The Churches were stepping into their own culture and redeeming the culture for Christ. This exploration was aided by younger leaders such as Leslie Shyllon, Francis Nabieu, Samuel Hanciles, Sahr Yambasu, Arnold Temple and others.

The Scripture Union movement was exercising a great influence for good among young people throughout the country and in all churches. In a country of 5 million people it was estimated that 20% were under the age of 19 years. Scripture Union leaders like Frank Tichy, Bill Roberts, Aureola Jones, Emerson Thomas, Billy Simbo and Musa Jambawai (Sierra Leone Fellowship of Evangelical Students) led camps and rallies for young people throughout the country and many met with Christ in a life-changing way. These young Christians were discipled and several would hear God's call to Christian leadership. Working alongside Bill Roberts were some mentors who were academics, including Dr Daniel Jonah, Dr Modupeh Taylor-Pearce, Dr Tony Powell and Mrs Paulina Powell, Marcus Pettman and Don Kinde. These impacted a generation of younger leaders encouraging them in biblical Christianity and to adhere to the fundamentals of the faith while doing mission differently. It was a time when all over the world, Pentecostal churches were growing. The charismatic movement was renewing worship in mainline European and American churches

The church was growing and so was Islam. Figures suggested that 30% followed traditional beliefs, 58% were Muslims and 12% were Christians. The figure seems small for Christians and some have pointed to the challenge of monogamy as an obstacle to faith. It can be said that although a small section of society, Christians were 'punching above their weight' not least because of the number of church schools, both primary and secondary.

The Wallaces worked hard. Occasionally they would visit the magnificent Lumley beach for a swim in the warm ocean. Would John Wesley the founder of Methodism have approved of a visit to the beach? He told his preachers: "Be diligent. Never be unemployed. Never be triflingly employed. Never while away time, nor spend more time at any place than is strictly necessary." On occasions when our family would come to Freetown on business, we would try to arrive

State House Presentation with H.E. Dr Siaka Stevens and H.E. President Julius Nwyere of Tanzania, 1980.

early in order to snatch an extra day or two for relaxation but Leslie would ask the awkward question: "When did you come down from the Provinces?"

Interesting visitors were always arriving in Freetown. In 1973 two contrasting people arrived in Freetown at different times. One was an unconventional American evangelist called Arthur Blessitt and the other was the renowned Bible teacher and author from London, Rev Dr John Stott. Arthur Blessitt arrived unannounced from California to carry a large ten foot wooden cross on a walk from Freetown to Nairobi. He had little idea of the climate and culture but was helped by Philip Cheale, Billy Simbo and others. Wherever Arthur Blessitt went, some thought him to be mad. Others thought he looked like Jesus and they followed him until he had to ask them to go back because they were hungry and he had no food to give them. He said it was like living in gospel times. He had no money but people in the villages and towns offered him hospitality. When he reached the Liberian border he still had three days left on his visa and Billy Simbo drove him to Koidu diamond mining area where he stayed with our family for three days and Frances bandaged his blistered feet. In Koidu thousands gathered in the school football fields for evangelistic rallies led by this off-beat but genuine man who came from the hippie culture of California but who was filled with the Spirit of Jesus his Saviour. He galvanised crowds by calling: "Give me a J; give me an E, an S, a U, an S – JESUS!" Many were converted including scores of young people, some of whom would become leaders. It was a demonstration of Christian mission being done differently.

By contrast, Rev Dr John Stott, who was on a lecture tour of West Africa, spoke more reflectively, though no less powerfully, at an inter-denominational Pastors' Conference where several hundred participants gathered to learn Expository Preaching. Dr Stott made a plea for biblical preaching and encouraged the preachers to be students of the word of God in order to guard the gospel against distortions. "To preach is to open up the inspired text with such faithfulness and sensitivity that God's voice is heard and God's people obey him" he explained. He encouraged "double listening" whereby we listen to the voice of the Spirit of God through the Bible and we listen to the cry of the needy world. He exhorted the preachers to look more like the Christ whom they were proclaiming because personal authenticity communicates more powerfully than words, though words are very important. He quietly prayed for the preachers to receive more of God's Holy Spirit in order to be more like Christ.

Another influential visitor was Miss Pauline Webb, a Vice-President of the World Council of Churches, an officer of the Mission House who sounded a prophetic voice among leaders of the World Church. Presidents of overseas Methodist Churches were among the many visitors including Rev Andrew Ndhlela of Zimbabwe, Rev Basil Rajasingham of Sri Lanka and Rev Dr Norman Taggart of Ireland.

In 1977 the gospel ship MV Logos arrived in Freetown and was well-received. Leslie played his part in facilitating the visit when many young people were converted and trained to share their faith. Another attempted military *coup* occurred at this time when Leslie was on board the MV Logos addressing the public and some security folk, fearing the consequences, turned off his public microphone.

These were busy times but Leslie never gave the impression of being overwrought. Agnes kept open house for numerous local and international visitors, both planned guests and stranded guests. Their home at Old Railway Line sometimes seemed like an international, interdenominational guest house. In one month they recorded 34

Fourah Bay College Graduation Ceremony

visitors. While Agnes and Leslie were always softly spoken, the fun was always wholesome. Truth only has to be whispered to be heard.

At a time of civil unrest in Freetown with some rioting on the streets, Leslie drove his car into the centre of the city and was surrounded by an angry mob. His watch and spectacles were stolen but he quietly remonstrated with the people until someone in the crowd recognised him and he was allowed safe passage.

On Christmas Day 1974 after a spate of attempted break-ins at his house, late at night some robbers entered the compound at his home and injured the watchman. Leslie told Agnes, who herself was unwell, to close the doors while he went out to rescue the watchman. Leslie was seriously wounded with a blow to the head which left him with a broken jaw, a serious injury to his eye socket and much bleeding. Agnes came looking for him in the dark and thought he might be dead. Getting medical attention on the night of Christmas was difficult and eventually he was admitted to Hill Station Hospital and the Connaught Hospital in Freetown. Two Methodist doctors who were close friends of Leslie attended him. They were Dr Roxy Harris, a consultant surgeon and Dr Ronnie Cummings, a dental consultant. As the word spread, the Freetown community was horrified at this attack. On the following day, the President of Sierra Leone, His Excellency Dr Siaka Stevens heard the news of the attack and came himself to Hill Station hospital to see Leslie and to enquire about his condition which was serious. The Head of State ordered that Leslie be flown to London and admitted to a Private hospital at the expense of the Sierra Leone Government.

Two leading Freetown laymen, E.J. Robinson and L.T.B. French were there to pray for him and to wave goodbye as he was taken on board the ferry to cross the bay to Lungi airport. His plane had to make an emergency landing in The Gambia where Leslie remembers sitting in pain under a tree at the airport while the plane was being checked. In London, his teeth were removed, his jaw was reset with wire and his eye socket repaired. An Irish Methodist minister, Rev Dr Norman Taggart and his wife Margaret were at that time attached to the Mission House in London and were very kind to Leslie and Agnes. The situation was aggravated when Verena, who at that time was a boarder in Methodist College, Belfast, received the message that her dad had been shot. When hospitalisation in London was over, Leslie called in to Leicester Square Dental hospital to say thank you to Professor Hay who had performed a succession of operations on his jaw.

At this time Agnes was admitted to another London hospital and diagnosed as having pernicious anaemia. It was a difficult time for the family but their trust in an all-knowing God gave them strength in their trials. I never heard him complain or even blame his attackers. He had already forgiven them, even though they remained unknown. He did not become pre-occupied with his own pain and although scarred for life, he regarded his brutal experience as an instance of a worldwide scar. He remembered that his Lord and Saviour suffered redemptively. He knew that others were facing the kind of injustice that he did.

On his return to Sierra Leone, Leslie made a personal courtesy call to State House to express his thanks. When the President of the Methodist Church was ushered in, The Head of State rose from behind his desk and greeted him with an embrace and the words: "Welcome Home, Mr President." Government thereafter placed a security guard on the manse. Relations with Dr Siaka Stevens were sometimes tense but respectful. Leslie was no 'palace priest' who curried favour with those in power. Sometimes, in true prophetic fashion he was a 'troubler of

Israel.' He was invited to preach the sermon at the annual Assize service in the presence of the Head of State, Cabinet ministers, the Lord Chief Justice and the robed judiciary. Sometimes such formal services were occasions when sermons were preached well while saying little. Leslie chose as his subject 'The value of the human being' and spoke of both the dignity and degradation of humanity. He warned about the evil of corruption which denied justice to the poor. He quoted the words of the prophet (Amos 5:24): "Let justice roll down like waters and righteousness like an ever-flowing stream." He let his audience know that what the world needs is not amazing power but amazing grace, the saving grace that comes from the Lord Jesus Christ and is freely given to all who seek it. Leslie was aware of a culture of corruption and believed that halting such oppressive practices was one reason for the mission of the church. On the next morning the Freetown *Daily Mail* had a large two inch headline in solid black print on its cover page: "WALLACE WARNS THE NATION." He kept his passport with him for the next few days in case he would be asked to leave the country. It was testimony to his acceptance as an expatriate in a post-colonial, independent nation that his words were heard. Leslie believed that the word of God has transforming effect.

On another occasion when there was talk about the purchase of a presidential jet for the Head of State, the university students and others were opposed to the idea. Leslie spoke with the Head of State and pointed out that Government grants were still owing to students and others who were being told that Government had no money. The jet was not purchased.

Other West African countries were changing their names from colonial titles. Gold Coast had become Ghana and Dahomey became Benin. Sierra Leone had been given its name in 1462 by the Portuguese explorer Pedro da Cinta. On his ship in the large natural harbour he saw the Freetown mountains and heard the roar of tropical thunder. He described the place as the: "land of the lion mountain." There was discussion about changing the name from Sierra Leone to the Republic of Songhai, an ancient West African kingdom. Again there was opposition to the cost of the change at a time of deprivation. The church leaders pointed out to the Head of State the financial implications of such a change at a time of economic stringency when teachers were not being paid and government grants owed.

Leslie was honoured by Her Majesty the Queen in 1975 when he was awarded the M.B.E. for services to the Commonwealth. The investiture was held at the British High Commission with church officials present. Such awards he would have preferred to keep secret but the Freetown *Daily Mail* produced another of its large bold headlines: "QUEEN HONOURS REV WALLACE."

In 1980, as a mark of the respect in which Leslie was held by the President and the country he was given a State honour at another ceremony in State House when he was installed as (C.R.) 'Commander of the Rokel.' This ceremony was attended by Dr Julius Nyerere, President of Tanzania who spoke of his appreciation of Christian mission work in his home country.

One of the most demanding situations in which he found himself was when students of Fourah Bay College demonstrated at a graduation ceremony attended by the Head of State, Dr Siaka Stevens. Leslie was a member of the University Council and was present at the formal ceremony at Fourah Bay in 1971. Dr Siaka Stevens had invited members of the diplomatic corps to be present with the intention of making an appeal for foreign funds to support the College, of which he was Chancellor. Some students in the crowd had secreted protest posters on their persons and when the Head of State began to speak they caused a disturbance and displayed posters insinuating State corruption, with such captions as: "Where is the Sierra Leone Diamond?" or "Who pays for the Presidential Jet?" Members of the Presidential bodyguard, the Internal Security Unit raised their weapons and Leslie implored them not to shoot. The dignitaries were ushered into the library until order was restored. It was a tense time when the University community felt under-funded. Dr Siaka Stevens never felt he had uncritical support from the students.

In the aftermath of this drama, the chair of the College Council appointed Leslie to preside over an investigation of the students' grievances. He met with many people especially student leaders and staff representatives. The staff was divided concerning the appropriateness of the student protest. The students had understandable grievances. When Leslie met the President of the Students' Council, the young Mr Sumner was uneasy until Leslie enquired about his mother's health. The

Some circuit stewards 1974.

student leader was surprised and Leslie explained that when his father Mr Doyle L Sumner, was a lecturer in Union College, Bunumbu, the young man, then a child, was taken ill. Leslie drove his father and the boy to the Methodist Hospital in Segbwema, where he recovered. After this, Leslie had fresh credibility with the students and heard their grievances which included concerns about lack of finance for the College, alleged corruption and issues of food hygiene. Leslie tried faithfully to present their grievances to the University Council and faced resistance from the College Principal. He remembers the committee met on Christmas Eve and on Boxing Day to finalise their report as speedily as possible. The report was duly presented in January to the College Council and broadcast on National radio. The next College graduation was held without incident. Upon reflection, this was an unenviable task for any person to undertake in a climate of distrust. Yet Leslie was 'a man for all seasons' and had the respect of students, the staff, the College Principal and The Head of State. It was most gratifying at the ensuing graduation ceremony at Fourah Bay College when one of the new graduates shook his hand and said: "Thank you, Sir. If it had not been for you, this day might have never come." Did not Jesus say: "Blessed are the peacemakers for they shall be called children of God?"

Why did Leslie, who is by nature quiet and self-effacing, get involved in public ministry at the heart of the capital city of the nation? He was living out a personal conviction. He believed in God. If the God with whom he walked and talked is indeed creator and sovereign over everything, then everything finds its identity and meaning in relationship to Him - not only our spiritual life but also our work, politics, science, education, the arts and all of human life. This was the Christian worldview which had long since caught his imagination and drawn from him total commitment in the cause of Jesus. Abraham Kuyper expressed this well when he said: "There is not a square inch in the whole domain of our human existence over which Christ . . . does not cry: 'Mine!'"

He is one of few pastors who likes administration. One year he counted the number of committees and Boards of Management that he chaired and they amounted to 34 Boards and Committees. He believed that committees were important to do detailed work. He gained satisfaction when committees actually achieved something instead of being 'talking shops.'

Before he retired from missionary service, Leslie received a letter from Rev Charles Eyre, Secretary of the Irish Methodist Conference, enquiring if he would make himself available for nomination for the post of President of the Methodist Church in Ireland. This generous consideration was quietly declined "because of commitments in Sierra Leone."

CHAPTER 12

INTER-CHURCH PROJECTS

Medical work

On the medical side of Church work, Leslie was a member and Chairperson on the Nixon Memorial Hospital Board of Management, which provided General Nurse Training, a Midwifery School, Nutrition Centre, under-five clinics and village clinics. It was beneficial in every way to promote a joint training programme with the Catholic Mission. Back home in Ireland there may have been tensions between Protestants and Roman Catholics, but here in Sierra Leone there was no time for that. Tutorial staff members were shared between the Serabu Catholic Hospital and the Methodist Hospital Segbwema, about one hundred miles apart. Sister Hilary was an Irish Catholic nun who was doctor and medical Superintendent at Serabu and she worked closely with Dr Len Wilkinson, the legendary Medical Superintendent at Segbwema and with his successors. Leslie was a founder member of the Board of CHASL, (Christian Health Association of Sierra Leone) which was an interdenominational umbrella group for church medical work. It was authorised to import medicines into the country in bulk and therefore at a cheaper rate than individual hospitals could command. As well as Segbwema Hospital there were several Methodist Clinics including those at Bunumbu, Sandaru and Koidu, which benefited from CHASL.

Theological Training

Training for ministers and members was a priority for the growing Church. In 1960s students for the ordained ministry were being trained at either Fourah Bay College Department of Theology (FBC) or at Sierra Leone Bible College, Jui (SLBC). A few persons were being trained outside of the country in Legon (Ghana), Ibadan (Nigeria) or Cliff College (England). Bible Colleges at Bunumbu and Segbwema or the Bible Training Institute at Bo continued to serve the needs of rural churches and vernacular training.

For several years the United Methodist Church, (UMC), the Methodist Church (MCSL) and the Sierra Leone Church (SLC), had felt the need for a training facility that would include training of ministers and members, providing a balance between theological education and church training. The leaders of these three denominations met on several occasions to discuss the matter and to pray about it. Archbishop Moses N C O Scott (Anglican,) Bishop Benjamin A Carew (UMC) and Dr W E A Pratt and Leslie (Methodist) explored the idea of training ministers and members at the one centre. Consideration had been given to the creation of such a facility at Bo (BTI) where Rev Eustace Renner was principal and at Jui (SLBC) where Rev Don Kinde was principal. These plans came to nothing.

In Freetown, Rev Professor Canon Harry Sawyerr of Fourah Bay College was initially hostile to any training programmes that could be construed as a breakaway from the college. The church leaders however were now seriously considering a separate institution to be called a 'Theological Hall and Church Training Centre'. The title indicated the vision that would provide a combination of academic theological teaching and practical skills in leadership and evangelism for ministerial and lay students. The church leaders visited several sites including Leicester Peak, Methodist City Mission in John Street, the UMC property on Circular Road and the Anglican property at Bishop's court.

By this time Rev Hugh E Thomas, an English Methodist minister experienced in Theological Training in Ghana was sent by the Methodist Church and appointed by the sponsoring denominations to help set up the new Theological Hall and Church Training programme. He launched the programme in several temporary locations. The first location was at Methodist City Mission, John Street. Classes were later moved to the old building of the Albert Academy, Berry Street, before continuing in Bishop's Court. The vision of a facility for theological and lay training was being realised and a more permanent site was required. The Methodist Church Trustees were approached concerning the

Freetown Ordination at Fort Street Pentecostal Church

renting of their premises adjacent to Wesley Street which had formerly been a campus of the Methodist Boys' High School. In England, the sale of Richmond College which formerly trained Methodist missionaries made possible a generous grant by the British Methodist Church through the Methodist Church Overseas Division (MCOD). This grant paid for the upgrading of the property, providing classrooms downstairs and two staff apartments upstairs for visiting lecturers. The Theological Hall and Church Training Centre now had premises fit for purpose. The three sponsoring churches would pay one third each of the running costs of the programme. They would provide staff quarters for their own staff and student accommodation for their own students. Students were appointed by their church bodies. Each denomination was expected to provide a member of staff.

The Rev Hugh E Thomas resided at Brookfields and he was joined by his successor Rev Canon Philip Ross. Rev Canon Philip Ross was an Anglican CMS missionary. He was an experienced theological teacher and his wife Betty was a lecturer in Greek. They encouraged in the students an enthusiasm for Bible study and evangelism. Scholarships and research places in British universities were awarded to some excellent students. Two of these students who went to study in Queen's University Belfast, were Rev Dr Sahr J Yambasu and later Rev

101

Francis Nabieu. Each would later take on the role of Principal of the Theological Hall and Church Training Centre. Methodist missionary Miss Monica Humble, an accomplished theologian joined the staff and she promoted Theological Education by Extension (TEE) and travelled throughout the country on public transport as she supervised students. The UMC in Moyamba District was one of the first areas to embrace the concept of TEE in those early years.

The Rev Professor Canon Harry Sawyerr CBE, who had retired from Fourah Bay College where he was Principal, came to serve as Principal of the Theological Hall and Church Training Centre. His appointment signified an interesting conversion after his initial opposition. Canon Sawyerr, though a high churchman, had a passion for Africa to be evangelised by Africans. A Creole, he had lived as a youth in Mendeland and based on his early experiences and later reading he wrote the book *Creative Evangelism* and *God, Creator or Ancestor*. Later the Rev Dr M Markwei was nominated by the UMC to be Principal and approached the task with enthusiasm. Rev Francis Nabieu was in charge of TEE at this time. After Dr Markwei, Rev Dr Sahr John Yambasu was appointed Principal and when he left in September 1995, Rev Francis Nabieu succeeded him. Rev Dr Olivia Wesley would become the first woman principal.

It was not only students from the mainline churches who were trained. Evangelical ecumenism was affirmed when two students from the Pentecostal (Limba) Church graduated from the Theological Hall and Church Training Centre. A unique ecumenical ordination service with the sacrament of the Lord's Supper was held in Fort Street attended by Bishop Bangura (UMC), Rev S L Wallace (MCSL) and Rev Professor Canon Harry Sawyerr (SLC).

Informal training was continuing in all Methodist circuits and Rev Dr Leslie Shyllon, although an academic, was meticulous and industrious in promoting leadership training at circuit level in Freetown. With the closing of the Bible School at Njaluahun, Rev Gilbert Hall at Kenema, with others, was promoting quality local preacher training.

The bringing to birth of the Theological Hall and Church Training centre came after a long gestation. Yet it would produce fruit because it was a God-given vision which was courageously nurtured by Godly church leaders and continues to serve the church and the Kingdom of God in Sierra Leone.

The Koidu Joint Parish (United Methodist and Methodist)

The Koidu Joint Parish was formed in the year 1970 on 1st July, as collaboration in mission in the Kono District, Sierra Leone between the United Methodist Church and the Methodist Church. Rev Dr Benjamin Carew (UMC Bishop) and Leslie as Methodist President were the driving force behind it.

The background to the story begins in 1952 when the Sierra Leone Selection Trust (SLST) Agreement with the Colonial government gave SLST the diamond mining rights for the whole of the country. Any diamonds found by citizens became the property of SLST without compensation. The churches lobbied Government for a change in the law in the interest of people who found diamonds on their own land. At Independence in 1961 the SLST boundaries were re-drawn. These alterations gave rise to a mass emigration to the Kono area from within and outside the country and the development of an illicit diamond mining boom. As early as 1955 the Methodist Church began talks with the Evangelical United Brethren about collaborative work in the Kono District.

The Evangelical United Brethren Church (later to become the United Methodist Church) had established evangelistic, educational and medical work throughout many parts of the Kono District. The Methodist Church work in the Kono District was limited to the Soa and Gbaneh Chiefdoms where it had expanded from the Sandaru Circuit in the Kailahun District in the 1950s. Ministers from both churches were occasionally invited to conduct Sunday Services at the Sierra Leone Selection Trust Mining Company Headquarters in Yengema.

In 1969 Rev Sidney Groves visited the area from Kenema and met with the Methodist diaspora including traders, Sierra Leone Selection Trust company employees as well as illicit diamond miners. They generally welcomed the idea of a Methodist mission in Koidu and in the mining camps. Also visited was Madam Bruce John, a Methodist trader in Koidu, originally from the Ebenezer Methodist Circuit in Freetown and then a church leader in the local United Methodist Church at Paul Square, Koidu. Mama John had the gift of prayer and healing and could speak in tongues. She welcomed the possibility of Methodist work in the town and surrounding area but felt torn between her Methodist roots and her UMC relationships in the Koidu Church. She famously made a plea to Sidney Groves: "Please do not divide me, let us have a joint mission in Kono" and this became the prophetic word for what would later become the Koidu Joint Parish. The vision seemed good to other local UMC church leaders including Mr K.T. Turner JP, the Head teacher of Koidu UMC Boys' School, and Chief S.A. Sinah and Mr Terry Bartlam who was Principal of Koidu UMC Secondary School. The Rev A. J. Smith, the UMC District Superintendent was acquainted with the proposal and had misgivings about the plan.

In Freetown, the report of Sidney Groves was given to the leadership of both the Methodist and UMC Conferences. The Rev Dr Benjamin Carew the UMC Bishop, Rev Clyde Gallow an American missionary with the UMC and Rev S. L. Wallace, President of the Methodist Church, met together in Freetown in the Methodist Church Headquarters building in 11 Gloucester Street and after prayer and reflection agreed that for Kono, mission together would be stronger than mission apart. Not everyone in each Conference was initially enthusiastic about joint work.

A Constitution was drawn up for the formation of a Koidu Joint Parish. The word 'Parish' was not commonly used at that time in either church tradition but the term was in use in the American UMC Constitutional documents and it also had the resonance of Rev John Wesley's utterance: "The world is my parish." So a fresh word for a fresh venture was deemed appropriate.

It was agreed that each Conference would supply a minister. Both Conferences would jointly support the work financially and if possible, in equal measure. Both parent bodies would receive regular progress reports, membership returns, financial statements and staffing updates. The membership returns were to be reported to the respective Conferences on a 50% basis. Existing links between Women's and Men's organisations and Youth Work would be retained with their parent bodies in both Conferences. The work of the UMC Boys' school and UMC Girls' school at Koidu, as well as the UMC schools at Penduma and Kwakoema would remain as UMC Schools but would come under Koidu Joint Parish management. It was agreed that the area of work was to cover Koidu-Sefadu, the outlying villages, the mining camps and other areas where there was no existing UMC work. The administration of the Koidu Joint Parish would be carried out through a local leaders' meeting. The oversight of the work would be the responsibility of a Koidu Joint Parish Council which was made up of The UMC Bishop and the Methodist President (as co-chairs), the Secretaries of both Conferences, the UMC District Superintendent of Kono and the Methodist District Chairman, the two ministers appointed to the Parish and two laypersons from the Parish. The meetings of the Council were normally held in Freetown.

The first ministers the Koidu Joint Parish were Rev David S M Bockari (UMC) and Rev Ken Todd (Methodist). David was a Kono and regarded Madam Bruce John as his mother-in-God. Each minister was provided with a parsonage or manse and with a vehicle. The carpenters were S M Jusu and Mr Mori. Sidney Groves and John Goatley supervised the transfer from Kenema to Koidu of a used, wooden, prefabricated house which became the Methodist mission house in the Koidu Secondary School compound. The hole for the underground cistern to hold rainwater was dug more deeply than required in the hope that the diggers might find a diamond.

Mr A N Dauda and Mr K T Kanawa were catechists. Rev Paul Dunbar, a retired UMC minister residing in Koidu was supportive. The new Joint Parish Church at Pimbi Lane, which could seat several hundreds, was opened in 1971 by Rev Dr Benjamin Carew (UMC Bishop) and Rev S L Wallace MBE (Methodist President). In the first eight years of the Koidu Joint Parish over 1000 adult believers were baptized. Two of these were medical doctors, Dr Fasuluku Suku-Tamba who later became Minister of Health and Dr Moiwo Korji who later became Minister of Information. Later Rev Dr Stephen Mosedale came from UK and his wife Dr Brenda Mosedale started the Koidu Joint Parish Clinic. Revs M.M. Pewa, Francis S Nabieu, Samuel Rogers, David Cole and Robbie Bowen were later appointed. In later years, two members were elected as Vice-President of the Methodist Conference, Mrs Mary Musa (who through illness was unable to take up her appointment) and Mrs Alice Bockerie-Torto JP.

It was always the hope of the founding fathers and mothers that the Koidu Joint Parish would set the pattern of further co-operation between the UMC and the Methodist Church. This hope still remains today.

CHAPTER 13

IRELAND – RETIREMENT

Celebrating 60 years of ministry with daughter Verena

Following the death of her father in 1974, Mrs Agnes Wallace remained in Belfast to care for he mother. Agnes later faced personal illness with bravery and faith. She was able to return to Sierra Leone and they both retired from overseas missionary service in 1987. When they were leaving the country which Leslie had accepted as his home for so long, Sierra Leone was still developing and needing international aid even though it had natural resources including diamonds, gold, iron ore, bauxite, rutile, palm oil, fish, coffee, and cocoa. The church was growing with fewer mission partners and more indigenous leadership. Many tears were shed at a succession of farewell occasions. At one of the farewell parties in Freetown he was referred to as 'a missionary hero' and as 'a history-maker'. It was more delightful to his ears to hear the comment: "Many have been brought to know the Lord Jesus as their Saviour and Friend by your presentation of the gospel in a style so clear and chaste, characterized always by tact and good taste, and often by sallies of brilliant wit."

They retired to Bangor, Northern Ireland, whence he had set out 39 years earlier.

Secretary of Methodist Missionary Society (Ireland)

On his return to Ireland he was appointed as Secretary of MMS in succession to Rev Ivan McElhinny. His colleagues were Rev Stanley Whittington (treasurer) and Harry Coote (Junior Mission for All). The office secretary was Mrs Agnes MacAuley who was followed by Mrs Joan Baird. The work of MMS (Ireland) continued to prosper and new ministries were supported. The 'Containers for World Mission and Development' programme had begun in the Lurgan Circuit by William Carson and others in response to the good work of Rev J Yedu Bannerman of Ghana. Containers are sent all over the world. Many were sent to Freetown in the aftermath of the rebel war when the Methodist Church Sierra Leone gave commendable leadership in the work of relief and development. During the rebel war Leslie was able to support extension work into Guinea and heard with great sorrow of the death of Rev T M Tengbeh while on a mercy mission there with people from Kailahun.

At this time MMS (Ireland) promoted VIM (Volunteers in Mission) teams started by Rev Denis Bambrick (formerly a mission partner in Ghana) and others. The first team had gone to Sierra Leone. The second team was called 'Back up Brazil' and the third was 'Go for Ghana.' Leslie participated in the Ghana team and worked at the Wenchi hospital for three weeks and Verena worked in Waa.

Leslie attended committees at a turbulent time in the Mission House in London where he sought to modify draconian changes to the overseas mission policy of the Methodist Church in Britain. He supported Rev Winston Graham, Mike King and other area secretaries whom he admired for the excellent leadership they gave to world mission. Rev Robert Russell subsequently took over as Secretary of MMS (Ireland).

In 1993, together with the Catholic Bishop of Liverpool, Bishop John Rawsthorne, Leslie was sent to Ethiopia on behalf of the Council of Churches of Britain and Ireland. It was a strategic visit to an ancient country with a troubled past. Quoted in his report are the words: "We

Honoured by the Northern Ireland Assembly for
contributions to World Development, 2010

thank God for the voice of Africa – the voice of pain and joy, of anguish
and hope – which we confess we have failed to heed properly in the
past."

In 2003, Leslie returned to Sierra Leone for a visit. To his surprise,
the Methodist Conference was postponed to coincide with his visit and
he was seated beside the President and the Secretary of Conference
and he was asked for words of wisdom from time to time. Rev Francis
S Nabieu was President. After Conference we were able to hitch a lift
in the helicopter of the United States Ambassador and Francis Nabieu,
Leslie and I were set down at Daru, near Segbwema. It was not long
after the ceasefire which had ended the rebel war. The destruction of
human life and property was painful to witness. Tears were shed for
slaughtered loved ones as we made our way by Landrover to Freetown
visiting shattered communities at Segbwema, Njaluahun, Kenema, Bo
and Tikonko. "When the guns are silent, the interest is gone. Soundless
poverty is killing many of our people and this is a stumbling block to the
stabilisation of the country. We want people who will come and walk

through the mud with us" (from a Report on Ethiopia for the Council of Churches of Britain and Ireland, co-written by Leslie Wallace). These words could be said of Sierra Leone in the aftermath of the 11 year rebel war which ended in 2002. On the tour of these war-torn areas, several schools and buildings had the name 'Wallace' in their titles. This fact was noted in silence with a wry smile. Back in Freetown, the welcome was overwhelming. Our gracious host in Freetown, during the 2003 visit, offered us kind hospitality in Lacs Guesthouse. The Head of State, President Ahmad Tejan Kabbah hosted a reception in his residence in honour of Leslie. Rev Niall Johnston organised a party in Freetown for Leslie's old friends.

Sadly, on Sunday 27th January 2008, Agnes Wallace passed peaceably home to God, in her own home with Leslie by her side. It was just a few days after her 85th birthday. At the funeral service, Leslie and Verena were supported by many from the world church family and greetings were received from friends in Sierra Leone. Agnes was devoted to her Saviour, the Lord Jesus Christ, in Whose blessed presence she now abides for ever.

In 2010 Leslie was honoured by the Northern Ireland Government for his contribution to World Development at a civic reception held in Belfast.

He is now the 'Father of the Conference' (the longest-serving minister) for both the Sierra Leone and Irish Methodist Conferences. He continues to fulfil his calling to serve the present age and at his home in Bangor has been visited by successive Methodist Presidents from Sierra Leone. He has much to remember with thankfulness to God. He has even more to anticipate as the Book of Revelation (chapter 7 verse 9) anticipates: "Then I looked and there before me was a great multitude that no one could count, from every nation, tribe, people and language, standing before the throne and in front of the Lamb. They were wearing white robes and were holding palm branches in their hands." As he wrote in his Ethiopian report:

"Tomorrow is God's day."

Appendix A
Curriculum vitae

Name:	Samuel Leslie Wallace MBE CR (Methodist Minister – Missionary)
Date of Birth	24 March 1921 at Belfast, Northern Ireland
Education:	Early education at Bangor, N Ireland
1926	Started attending Queen's Parade Methodist Church, Bangor
1935-1942	Studied Typography and Graphic Arts at Belfast College of Technology, and employed in the printing trade
1942	Qualified as Local Preacher - Queen's Parade Circuit (Carnalea)
1939-1942	Served as member of Bangor Hospital Stretcher Party
1942-1944	Church Evangelist – Castlewellan and Annalong (Dundrum and Newcastle Circuit)
1944	Entered the Methodist Ministry from Newcastle and Dundrum Circuit
1944	1st July appointed as Pre-Collegiate Probationer to Dublin at Ringsend and Sandymount
1945	Probationer Minister at Waterford (Dungarvan) Circuit
1946	In July and August he supplied the Cork Circuit
1946-1949	Edgehill Theological College, Belfast and missionary training. Taught Bible Knowledge at Methodist College Belfast
1 Sept 1949	Sent to Sierra Leone as a Methodist Missionary – served at Bunumbu
10 Nov 1949	Seconded to The Gambia where the only two ministers had died. Acted as Secretary of Synod
14 Oct 1950	Appointed to Bunumbu and Bandajuma Yawei, Sierra

	Leone; Chaplain to Union College; Secretary Mende Area Council; Assistant Synod Secretary, Sierra Leone District
1951	In month of June, Ordination at Irish Conference whilst on furlough
1951-1956	Appointed as Superintendent of Kailahun Circuit for village evangelism, Primary school management and the development of Secondary schools
1956	Assistant Secretary West African Conference (African) Committee
1957	Methodist Missionary Society's Representative, Sierra Leone
1956-1967	Director of the United Christian Council Literature Bureau and Bunumbu Press; (National Adult Literacy Programme)
25 June 1958	Married Agnes Thompson in Mountpottinger Methodist Church, Belfast
27 April 1961	Independence for Sierra Leone after more than 150 years of British Colonial rule
16 July 1961	Birth of daughter Verena
1967	Superintendent of the Bo-Tikonko Circuit
21 Jan.1967	Secretary of Inaugural Conference of the Methodist Church, Sierra Leone. Drafted the Constitutional Practice and Discipline of the Conference
19 Jan 1968	Appointed Officiating Chaplain to the Republic of Sierra Leone Military Forces (OD) Freetown Area
1 Sep 1968	Superintendent the Mende City Mission, Freetown
1968	Vice-President of the Boys' Brigade Executive, Sierra Leone
1 Nov 1968	Appointed visiting Chaplain to Prisons
1970-1974	President of the Conference of the Methodist Church, Sierra Leone

1971	Member of the University College Council
15 Dec 1971	Appointed Chairman of Committee investigating Student complaints and disturbances at Fourah Bay College, University of Sierra Leone
1974	Member of Court, University of Sierra Leone
1974-1977	President of the United Christian Council
1975	Acting President of Conference
1975	Appointed a Member of the Order of the British Empire, MBE
1976-1980	President of Conference (5 years)
1976-1980	Chairman Board of Management, Nixon Memorial Methodist Hospital
1980	Appointed Commander of the Rokel (Civil Division) Sierra Leone
	Chairman of Boards of Governors Methodist Secondary Schools:The Methodist Boys' High School, Freetown; The Methodist Girls' High School, Freetown; Wesley Secondary School, Segbwema; Njaluahun Girls; Bunumbu; Tikonko; Kenema; Kailahun
	Chairman Tikonko Agricultural Extension Centre Board of Management
	Member of the World Methodist Council Executive
	Chairman of the Council of the Methodist Church in West Africa
	Kailahun and Kissi Integrated Project
1981-1985	Secretary of Conference, Sierra Leone
1986-1987	President of Conference, Sierra Leone (1 year)
1987	Left Sierra Leone, prior to retirement from missionary service

1987	Assisted as supply minister at Carnalea Methodist Church, Bangor
1988-1996	General Secretary of Methodist Missionary Society (Ireland)
2008	Death of Mrs Agnes Wallace, 27th January 2008
2010	Honoured by the Northern Ireland Government for services to World Development

Appendix B

ADDRESS presented to
Revd. Samuel Leslie Wallace, C.R., M.B.E.

Ex-President of Conference of the
Sierra Leone Methodist Church

At Buxton Memorial Methodist Church, Charles Street, Freetown, on Sunday, 30th August, 1987 on the occasion of his retirement from Missionary Service in Sierra Leone

Dear Brother Wallace,

Your Day of toil with us for over 38 years has taught us that it is easier to say welcome than to say goodbye, a prospect which we now tacitly face.

We the members of the Methodist Church Sierra Leone, gather at this thanksgiving of prayer and praise, for the work and example you have shared with us. We also at this service recall the memory of a loved one and present to God one who has done more for us as a Church, than most of your immediate predecessors have done; one whose name will ever stir, like a trumpet, the hearts of every Sierra Leonean Christian, Methodist or non-Methodist.

As we reflect on your missionary exploits in virtually all Circuits of our three Districts, we recognise with relish your faithful studying of all details of your ministerial vocation, guided and inspired by that ever present sense of duty which was the most marked characteristic of your life.

As you prepared us for autonomy in 1966, you seem never to have entertained any doubt in your mind as to what God wanted you to do in 1967, in blending that your happy conjunction of great merit with your good fortune, which ultimately attended you the veteran missionary, already famous, and soon to win a nation-wide fame for your skill and daring enterprise in being the architect for our Autonomy as Primus Secretary of Conference.

Indeed in the whole exercise, we were able to see that if nerve made the man, you were already as good as made at that point in time of our Church's history. In you the fame of missionary heroes, as read in books, pragmatically captivated and charmed the imagination of Sierra Leoneans of all ages.

Many have been brought to know the Lord Jesus as their Saviour and Friend by your presentation of the gospel in a style so clear and chaste, but pregnant and pointed, characterized always by tact and good taste, and often by sallies of brilliant wit.

You have made history that would take a gigantic task to surpass when you became President of the Methodist Church on three different occasions or terms. It was neither a luck accident, nor an ecclesiastical favour, nor simply by growing old in the ministry, that you were honoured on all these three occasions with the high office of a President with its attendant responsibility. The fact is that it was realised by all in authority that you had put your conscience into your work as well as in the least details as in the great principles of our work. You were ordained and we watched you rise in rank and status, and never once were you found unequal to any task imposed upon or assigned to you.

Much as a Church we owe it to your matchless service, which your brain and courage rendered in our days of missionary dependence and struggle, we are still more indebted to you for the unconditional loyalty of your large and generous heart.

You have relentlessly worked as our Army Chaplain (other denominations), with our youths in the Boys' Brigade and the Ex-Service Men's Association; but you will be much remembered as a prison Chaplain of our Central Prison, where you have demonstrated that the great element of reform is not born of human wisdom but is found only in Christianity. By your mission to prisoners, the ignorant and poor alike of all creeds and even no creeds, you endeavoured to show us with what an eye this your faith regards the lowest and least of our race; and by this faith you have let the human soul live in harmony with the divine will so that in rehabilitation this earth would become like heaven. You demonstrated great faith in human progress with a confidence in reform. Thus your faith in reform is indissolubly connected with all that is hopeful, spiritual, capable in man. The example you have left us in this area of your ministry is what philanthropy can do when imbued with the spirit of Jesus.

We shall be remiss in our expression of thanks and appreciation if we leave out your wife Agnes and your daughter Verena who have suffered inconveniences at times as they toiled on without you at your native homeland Ireland, and would join you at their earliest convenience with charm and gladness. All we can say tonight, for lack of adequate words to express our appreciation, is that we devoutly join with the Wallace family, both present here and absent, in thanksgiving to Almighty God that He has spared the honoured life of you Leslie, and vouchsafed to you the glory of this day.

The heavens over you are the same, the shores that landed you 38 years ago are still here, morning comes and evening as they did and so shall always be our memories of you and your family – evergreen. This shall be so, because your leading characteristics are eminent piety and vigour of intellect, keenness of logic, burning power and plainness of language, whether English or Mende, melting pathos, cloudless perspicuity, graceful description, and a certain vehemence of feeling which brings home your words with an irresistible force.

As we wish you farewell, shall we have another Leslie Wallace, whether at home or from overseas to inspire us? Will your colleagues and other future ministers share your devotion to duty, your courage and faith? Yes, on this one condition, that every Methodist child learn from his or her cradle, as you Leslie Wallace no doubt learned from your cradle, that his or her first and last duty is to his or her Lord Jesus Christ the Church and this nation, and that to live for the Methodist Church in honour, and to die for her is glory.

Go in peace and the God of all peace be with you.

Yours faithfully

The document is signed by twelve officers of the Methodist Church, Sierra Leone as follows:

Gershon F H Anderson (President of Conference)

John Davies (Vice President of Conference)

S Dowridge Williams (Secretary of Conference)

Leslie Ephraim Shyllon (Chairman, Western District)

E L Coker (Conference Treasurer)

George Y Macauley (Chairman Bo-Kenema District)

Francis S Nabieu (Chairman Kailahun-Kono District)

Valentine Agbaje (President Women's Work)

Charles Williams (President MAYC)

M Selinga (Provincial District Women's Fellowship)

C Taylor (President Methodist Laymen's Association)

Olayinka Doherty (Sunday School Representative)

Appendix C

List of Presidents of the Sierra Leone Methodist Church

Rev Dr W E Akinumi Pratt OBE MA

Rev S Leslie Wallace CR MBE

Rev P A J Williams

Rev S Leslie Wallace CR MBE

Rev Nelson H Charles

Rev S Leslie Wallace CR MBE

Rev Gershon F H Anderson

Rev S Dowridge Williams BD

Rev Christian V Peacock BA

Rev Francis S Nabieu MA

Rev Arnold C Temple MPhil MLitt

Appendix D

Chronological list of Sierra Leonean ministers
until Autonomy 1967

Joseph Wright	1844	Solomon J Davies	1887
Charles Knight	1844	Michael C French	1889
George H Decker	1848	Theophilus A Smith	1889
Joseph May	1848	Johannes L Davies	1893
Philip Wilson	1856	William B Marke	1894
James Hero	1857	Moses E Garber	1895
Charles Marke	1858	John R Frederick	1896
Daniel W Thorpe	1858	William C Lawrence	1896
York F Clement	1863	William G Nicol MA	1896
Samuel T King	1869	J H Pratt MA	1896
J Claudius May FRGS	1875	Theophilus A Faux	1897
Samuel W Davies	1876	D Boyle Reach	1897
Adam P Woods	1876	J Shonaveh Wright	1898
William G Marke	1876	James T Roberts	1902
David A John	1877	Moses F Samuels	1903
Theophilus A George	1879	James O E Taylor	1904
Lewis J Leopold	1879	Josiah N Pratt	1905
Joseph C Thomas	1880	Solomon Williams	1905
Emence G G Sutton	1881	Elkanah T Fyle	1907
Samuel T Peacock	1883	Emeric J E Dauphin	1908
John E Williams	1884	Charles L Leopold MA	1908
Moses W Randall	1885	Thomas C Parker	1912
Festus H Johnson	1887	J C O During MA BD	1913
Peter P Hazeley	1887	Eliab J T Harris	1917
Philip Johnson	1887	M D Thomas	1918

M W Cole BA	1918	Abayomi B Cole MBE	1960
C C Taylor	1918	Walter Williams	1961
Herbert Thomas MA	1920	S E L Duro Belford	1961
S H A Taylor	1920	I S A Paul-Coker	1966
D C Webber	1921	Leslie E T Shyllon BA	1966
D D A Cummings	1921		
E W B Cole MBE MA	1922		
E K E Williams MA	1923		
W E A Pratt OBE MA	1924		
T J Vivian Campbell BA	1924		
H L Forde MA	1928		
E A E Cole	1935		
Jeremiah Jedekiah Pratt	1935		
Charles J Smith	?		
Ola E K Ferguson	1940		
C S G Cole	1942		
James I Johnson	1942		
C Thomas Newstead	1943		
Prince A J Williams	1946		
W Byron Pratt	1948		
S Dowridge Williams BD	1952		
David M Karanke	1952		
Philip F Jibao	1955		
Samuel M Musa	1955		
Daniel D Tucker	1955		
Gershon F Anderson	1956		
M Collingwoode Johnson	1958		
Zacariah J Macauley	1958		

Appendix E

Lists of some missionary acquaintances recalled by Leslie, who lived and worked in Sierra Leone

Ministers

Edward Avery; Warren Bardsley; Robbie Bowen; Stanley Brown; Dwin Capstick; Leslie R Clarke; Peter Clark; Stuart Clarke; W R E Clarke; Harold T Cook; John Cree; Kenneth Crosby; Chris Eddy; John Goatley; David Griffiths; Sidney N Groves; Roger Grundy; Gilbert Hall; W Tom Harris; Raymond Hawthorne; Frank Himsworth; Richard Jackson; F Norman Jasper; Ray Johnston; Tom Johnston; Ray B Jowett; Moira Kerr-Shaw; A C Lamb; J R S Law; Roger Larkinson; Brian Lewis; Glanville T Magor; Francis Marratt; Henry N Medd; Stephen Mosedale; Ken Nicholson; Bob Priestley; Keith Parsons; Ewart Prickett; Bill Ream; Peter Rule; Christopher Shreeve; Roger H Smith; A Stott; Hugh E Thomas; Richard Thompson; S Kenneth Todd; Neil Trainer; F G Tucker; Arthur Wade; John Wallace; S Leslie Wallace; J J Whitfield; Denis Williams; Eric Wright; Gordon Wynne

Wesley Deaconesses

Celia Cotton; Mary Mawson; Joan Bardsley; Janet Marley

Administrators

included Vera Adams; Elma Burness; Violet Martin

Some medical and nursing missionaries who served in Nixon Memorial Methodist Hospital and in other clinics

Dr Colin Adey; Dr J L Avery; Miss U Baker; Sheila Baldwin; Joy Bannister; Dr Bell; Lily Benn; Dr Philip Brackenbury; Dr James Bunn; Dr L M Carter; Dr John Cochrane; Dr Roger Coles; Ivy Cook; Geoff Crawford; Dr Every; Elsie Fielding; Barbara Figg; Dr Jenny Gibson; Dorothy Green; Dr Mary Groves; Daisy Harris; Dorothy Heap; Dr Egbert Hopkins; Gertrude Hughes; Dr Carole Jackson; Miss Jebb; Dr Elizabeth Johnson; Dr Peter Johnston; Sybil Jones; Dr J Kearney; Dr Isabel King; Dr D Knights; Elizabeth Lyons; Alice Medd; Edith Milner; Dr Brenda Mosedale; Nan Mumford; Dr E Murphy; Keith

Parsons; Dr Roger Peppiatt; Dr Phillips; Dr Frances Price; Dr Michael
Price; Dr Nancy Ridley; Olly Robertson; Dr John Rose; Dr Sanderson;
Dr E Simpson; G I Smith; Glenys Smith; Olive Smith; Joyce Sorfleet;
Dr H Souster; Dr Stephenson; Dr Ken Strong; Mrs Strong; Dr Temple;
Joanna Tettey; Linda Turnbull; Frances Todd; Margaret Todd; Mary
Turner; Dr C deVoile; S van der Graaf; Dr Way; Dr P O Wakelin;
Barbara Walls; Marcia West; Mary Whitethread; Dr Len Wilkinson;
Win Wilkinson; Dr Joses Yuan

Notes:

The infant son of Rev H N Medd and Mrs Alice Medd died at the
age of one month and was buried in the Mission Compound at
Segbwema.

Sister Ivy Cook, who was in charge of Midwifery training, died in
Segbwema Hospital and was buried in the town.

Dorothy Heap died in Sierra Leone.

Dr Howard Souster later was elected as Vice-President of the British
Methodist Conference.

Barbara Walls became a Methodist minister upon return to the UK.

Some missionary teachers

Linda Adey; Irene Aldridge; Dena Atkins; Win Bairstow; Dr J R
Burne; Eileen Burton; Peter Byass; Margaret Byass; Ruth Capstick;
Janice M Clark; Mrs W R E Clarke; Marion Copithorne; Elaine Cox;
Peter Dear; Margaret George; Margaret Goatley; Hilda Gray; Evelyn
Green; Sybil Green; Sylvia Griffiths; Joan Grundy; Stanley Hall;
Sylvia Hall; Miss J Higman; Sheila Himsworth; F Alan Hopkins; T
G Hughes; Monica Humble; Frank Jasper; I Paul Jesudasan; Mike
King; Miriam J Knowles; Rachel Larkinson; Ken Lindsay; Janet
McCall; Malcolm McCall; Jill Morris; Mrs Newton; Allison Oliver;
Joan Parkin; Tom Patton; Derek Polley; Tanya Polley; Monica (Jervis)
Rhead; Peter Rule; Norah Senior; John Sergeant; Alan Shaw; Margaret
Thompson; Margaret Trainer; Margaret Turner; Margaret Wallace;
Andrew F Walls; Mrs Walmsley; Constance Worrall.

Notes:

Mike King (Njaluahun) later exercised a strategic role in the World Church Office in London where he was appointed Team Leader. In 2012 he would be elected Vice-President of the British Conference.

Miss Dena Atkins taught in Freetown Methodist Girls' High School before becoming a lecturer in Sir Milton Margai Teachers Training College.

Ken Lindsay (Kailahun) would return to Ireland, be ordained and be elected President of the Irish Methodist Conference for 2012.

Malcolm McCall (Kailahun) would return to England, be ordained and assist in the Cliff College International Training Centre.

Professor Andrew F Walls (Fourah Bay College) is a theologian and missiologist and a leading authority on the history of the African church.

Other mission personnel included: Bob Mann (Agriculture); Tony Cox (Youth); Michael Moss (Youth Work); Muriel Thomas (Training); Bob Dixon (Agriculture); Mike Humphries (Accountant); Aart Quak (Agriculture); Tim Brett; Brian Nixon; Wendy Juby (Administration); Dr Sleight (Educational development); Ted Moule (Hospital Administration); E Walton (Hospital Administration); A P Green (Hospital Administration); Mr Baker (Hospital Administration); A Dunwell (Builder); Michael Tettey (Hospital Administration); Mary Senior (Pastoral).